PUT IT IN WRITING
Second Edition

David Blot
Hostos Community College
City University of New York

David M. Davidson
Bronx Community College
City University of New York

NEWBURY HOUSE PUBLISHERS
A division of HarperCollins*Publishers*

Director: Laurie E. Likoff
Production Coordinator: Cynthia Funkhouser
Text Design Adaptation and Cover Design: Catherine Gallagher
Text Art: Heidi King
Compositor: Waldman Graphics
Printer and Binder: Malloy Lithographing Inc.

Text credits: "A Fallen Star Rebounds at Age 37," by Paul Finebaum, *The New York Times*, February 2. © 1986 by The New York Times Company. Adapted by permission. "Growing Up and Parenting": Thanks to Carmen Medina and Jose Cruz Matos of Hostos Community College, CUNY, for the idea behind this exercise. "Brief Encounter": from "New York Day by Day," by Susan Heller Anderson and David W. Dunlap, *The New York Times*, October 7. © 1985 by The New York Times Company. Adapted by permission. "Restoring Hispanic Theater in the Bronx," by Larry Rohter, *The New York Times*, January 12. © 1986 by The New York Times Company. Adapted by permission. "To Suffer a Prolonged Illness or Elect to Die," by Andrew H. Malcolm, *The New York Times*, December 16. © 1984 by The New York Times Company. Adapted by permission.

Photo credits: © Hervé Donnezan/Photo Researchers, Inc., page 2; Joe Greene, pages 5, 47, 60, 66, 73, 74, 75, 76; Ray Ellis/Photo Researchers, Inc., page 18; Van Bucher/Photo Researchers, Inc., page 68; Movie Star News, 134 West 18th St., New York, NY 10011, phone (212) 620-8160, page 91 (Linda Lavin); United Press International, page 91 (Danny Kaye).

NEWBURY HOUSE PUBLISHERS
A division of HarperCollins*Publishers*, Inc.

 Language Science
Language Teaching
Language Learning

Put It in Writing, Second Edition

Library of Congress Cataloging in Publication Data

Blot, David
    Put it in writing / David Blot, David M. Davidson.—2nd ed.
      p.   cm.
    ISBN 0-06-632137-9
    1. English language—Textbooks for foreign speakers.   2. English
language—Composition and exercises.   I. Davidson, David M.
II. Title.
[PE1128.B593 1988]
808'.042—dc19   88-4385
ISBN: 0-06-632137-9

63-20410   90 89 88 9 8 7 6 5 4 3

To Yolanda, Kay and Deborah
and
To the memory of Charles A. Curran

CONTENTS

MOVING ON

INTRODUCTION

This second edition of *Put It in Writing*, undertaken some seven years after the original publication, seeks to respond to three major concerns of teachers and administrators who have used and evaluated the book. First, it expands the range of use, providing more controlled writing exercises for high-beginning and low-intermediate students. This will give easier entry into the book for those students who may have completed a first ESL course, but who need additional work with a fair degree of control. There is also a new section, entitled "Moving On," designed to provide a transition for the advanced-intermediate student from the predominantly descriptive/narrative mode to expository writing. This last section seeks to involve students in thought and discussion about some larger social issues, and to help them bridge the thinking and writing gap between personal experiences and issues and those that affect a greater number of people.

A second concern was the need for more oral preparation for writing. This has been accomplished by the inclusion of exercises in which students can interact with both the material presented and their classmates, thereby developing ideas and gaining oral practice with words and structures that can facilitate a sounder and more satisfying writing experience. While this was the intent of the original edition, it has been made more explicit by the inclusion of sharing activities, such as retelling, interviewing, and guided group discussion at the start of virtually every selection.

Finally, the authors have responded to the concerns of those who appreciate the goals and content of the book but who, through lack of teaching experience and/or familiarity with the Counseling–Learning/Community Language Learning model, feel unable to use it effectively. In addition to the clarification of oral activities described above, an appendix entitled "From Teacher to Teacher" suggests ways to use the book, how to overcome potential difficulties, and ways to evaluate students' writing. With the use of guidelines and examples, we trust it will make *Put It in Writing* more accessible to more teachers.

In addition, the authors hope that "From Teacher to Teacher" will facilitate a two-way line of communication and welcome comments and questions regarding any aspect of the book.

Put It in Writing came into being as a result of the authors' work with college level ESL students at Bronx Community College and also their experience with Charles A. Curran's Counseling–Learning/Community Language Learning model.

The activities in the book go beyond being "high interest" materials. They encourage student investment because they each contain some idea, experience, or situation that students value. Students invest themselves because the activity somehow touches them and their lives.

Students write better when the "I" is involved, for example, as when (1) the student writes about him/herself in response to "My Life" or "Chi Lin's Escape to Freedom"; (2) the student writes about another person or an event but shows the relationship of that person or event to him/herself, as in "Uncle Carmine" or "The Grocery Store"; (3) the student writes about a person, situation, or event that he or she has no relationship to but gets personally involved with because of the inherent values. For example, with "Anna and Martin," a student may not be married or, if married, may not be facing the conflict that Anna and Martin are facing; nonetheless, a female student can value Anna's desire for more independence while a male student can value, or at least understand, Martin's feelings about being head of the household.

In the appendix, "From Teacher to Teacher," we explain in some detail how to use this book. We make just one fundamental point here: The teaching of grammar should be subordinate to the writing activity. If students begin with writing, then engage in a combination of correction and follow-up grammar, spelling, and vocabulary activities as needed, they are more likely to learn from their mistakes and to retain what they learn. In other words, the starting point is self-invested students entering into the writing activity. Their engagement causes them to be more open to, and to pay more attention to, the help the teacher gives them during and after the writing. They are more open because they value what they are writing and want to do the best they can.

To use this book as the authors intended, the writing must not be perceived by the students as their response to the teacher's grammar lesson; rather the grammar, spelling, and vocabulary activities must be seen as the teacher's response, after the fact, to the students' original investment in the writing. Proceeding this way frees the teacher to truly meet student needs.

The materials in *Put It in Writing* have been used with excellent results for more than ten years now in a variety of settings throughout the United States and abroad. Experience tells us that the book is most appropriate for older teenagers and adults whose abilities range from low-intermediate to low-advanced. *Put It in Writing* has become a standard text in certain high school ESL programs, adult ESL community programs, EFL courses, and a number of two- and four-year colleges. We hope that this second edition will continue to meet the needs of those programs as well as find a wider audience as a result of its substantial additions and revisions. We welcome your response to our efforts.

David Blot
David M. Davidson

SEMI-CONTROLLED WRITING

PROFILE

MELANIE WINSOME

HOME: Sydney, Australia; Beverly Hills, California; New York City; and wherever work and relationships take me.

AGE: 24

PROFESSION: Television actress.

HOBBIES: Sports, travel, reading, helping others, and enjoying good food.

LAST BOOK READ: *Jane Fonda's Workout Book.*

LATEST ACCOMPLISHMENT: Organized a tennis tournament for poor kids in Los Angeles.

WHY I DO WHAT I DO: Because life is for living and giving.

PERSONALITY: Enthusiastic, enterprising, communicative. Has a real talent for getting other people to enjoy and help themselves.

HER FAVORITE PUBLICATION: *MS Magazine.* "Ultimately, it may be the feminine outlook that saves the world."

PROFILE

ACTIVITIES

1. *With a partner.* Tell about yourself using the following categories. Then, write out your own profile.

   My home:
   My age:
   My profession:
   My hobby:
   Last book that I read:
   Last movie that I saw:
   My latest accomplishment:
   Why I am going to school:

   Brief description of my personality:

   My favorite newspaper or magazine and a comment about it:

2. *By yourself.* Using the information above, write a paragraph about yourself.

3. *With your partner or group.* Tell how you would like to be ten years from now, using the following categories. Then, *by yourself,* fill in the profile.

   My home:

   My age:

   My profession:

   My hobby:

My family:

Brief description of my personality:

4. *By yourself.* Pretend it is ten years from now. Using the information above, write a composition about yourself and tell how you are different from the way you were ten years ago. Also answer the following questions: What has been the biggest change in your life in the past ten years? Are you happier now? What helped you to change?

THE PERSON WHO TAKES CARE OF YOUR BUILDING

This is a story about the person who takes care of a house or building where more than one family lives.

ACTIVITY

With a partner. Write about the person who takes care of your (or someone else's) building or house. You may give additional information and examples.

Begin your story this way:

_The person who takes care of our building/house is called the *_____. His/Her name is _____._

Is the person who takes care of your building a man or a woman? How old is he/she? Is he/she married or single? Does he/she live in the basement or on one of the floors of the building or house? Does he/she speak English or some other language? Is he/she a friendly or an unfriendly person?

Does the * keep the building or house clean, or does he/she let it get dirty? Does he/she allow children to play near the building? In winter, does he/she provide enough heat? When something is broken, does he/she fix it or does he/she call someone in to repair it? Does he/she take care of the garbage or does he/she let it pile up?

Do the tenants like the * or not? Do they give him/her gifts on holidays?

*super
 superintendent
 janitor
 landlord
 concierge

6

MARIE CASTELLI

ACTIVITIES

1. *With a partner*. Write about Marie Castelli. You and your partner decide what details you want to include in the first and second paragraphs of your story. Both of you write exactly the same thing on your papers. When you have finished, check each other's papers to make sure that you have written the same thing and that there are no errors.

2. *By yourself*. Write your own ending to the story (third paragraph). Compare this ending with your partner's. Tell your partner why you decided to end the story this way.

1st para.

Marie Castelli: Born Naples, Italy, May 14, 1968.

Her parents: poor; father—a baker; mother—a housewife with _____children.

What kind of neighborhood did she live in? She liked her neighborhood. Why? Where did she play? Whom did she play with?

What kind of elementary school did she go to? Her teachers—good or bad? Classmates—friendly or unfriendly? What were her favorite subjects?

2nd para.

September 1982. Marie—high school. What was her major subject? Why? Who was her best friend? What did they do together?

Marie's mother died in 1983. What did Marie's father ask her to do? What did Marie decide to do? Was she happy or unhappy with her decision? Why?

3rd para. What happened to Marie when she was 19?

A DIFFICULT DECISION

This is a story about Edward, a young man who had to make a very difficult decision.

ACTIVITIES

1. *With a partner*. Write about Edward. You and your partner decide what details you want to include in the first and second paragraphs of your story. Both of you write exactly the same thing on your papers. When you have finished, check each other's papers to make sure that you have written the same thing and that there are no errors.

2. *By yourself*. Write your own ending to the story (third and fourth paragraphs). Compare your ending with your partner's. Tell your partner why you decided to end the story this way.

1st para.

Where does Edward come from?
- Greece
- Colómbia
- Japan
- Puerto Rico
- _____

How old is he?

When did he come to the United States?
- four years ago
- eight months ago
- when he was eighteen
- _____

Why did he come to the United States?
- He wanted to study.
- He wanted a better life.
- He wanted to make a lot of money.
- He wanted to escape oppression in his own country.
- He wanted to find a wife.
- _____

Edward was doing well in this country. Why?
- He was studying at a good college and was going to graduate in one year.
- He had a high-paying job with a chance for promotion.
- He was planning to marry a wonderful American woman.
- _____

2nd para.

But then something happened.

When did Edward receive a phone call?

Who was the phone call from?
- his father
- his mother
- his sister
- his fiancée
- _____

What did this person tell him?
- that his mother was very sick and needed his help
- that his father had cancer and needed his help
- that his fiancée was going to marry another man
- _____

3rd para.

What did this person want Edward to do?

What did Edward decide to do?

Why was this decision difficult for him?

What did he do after he made the decision?

4th para.

How do you feel about Edward's situation?

What do you think? Did he make the right decision? Why or why not?

MY NEIGHBORS

ACTIVITIES

1. *Interview*. Ask your partner to tell you about his/her neighbors. Then you tell your partner about yours. The questions below will help you.

2. *By yourself*. Write about your neighbors. You may give additional information and examples.

a. Who are your neighbors? (What are their names?) Do they live next door to you, across the street from you, or in the same building? Are they young, middle-aged, or older people? Are they friendly with everybody in the neighborhood or unfriendly? When you see them, do you talk to them or ignore them?

b. Do your neighbors keep their house or apartment clean or dirty? Are they quiet people, or are they always making a lot of noise? Do they mind their own business, or are they always talking about other people? Do they invite people to their house, or do they stay by themselves all the time?

c. Do you like or dislike your neighbors? Do you hope that they will continue to be your neighbors for a long time, or do you wish that they would move away?

MOVING

ACTIVITY

With a partner. Write this story. Using the choices given, you and your partner decide what you want to write. Write three paragraphs. Each of you write on your own paper. When you have finished, exchange papers and help each other to correct any errors that you find.

1st para.

Have Dennis and his wife decided to move to the suburbs
because they want to escape from all the problems of the city?
because Dennis has gotten a raise and he can afford to buy a house?
because their children are growing and they need a bigger place?
because they prefer suburban life to city life?

Have they started looking for a house
in the suburbs? (Which community?)
in another part of town? (Where?)
in another city? (Which one?)

Have they
spoken to several real estate agents?
read the classified ads in the newspaper?
driven around looking for houses with "For Sale" signs?

Did they spend _____ looking at houses?
last Saturday
last Sunday
all last weekend
the last two weekends

2nd para.

So far, they haven't found a suitable house
because all the houses they have seen have only one bedroom.
because all the houses they have seen are too expensive.
because the real estate agents won't show them houses in nice neighborhoods.
because Dennis/Dennis's wife is very fussy.

They aren't discouraged
because they know that finding a nice home takes time.
because they aren't in a hurry to move.
because they know that God will help them find the right house.
because they enjoy the excitement of making a major change in their lives.

3rd para.

Next week, what will Dennis and his wife continue to do?

THE FORTUNE TELLER

You are at a party and an interesting-looking person comes up to you and offers to tell your future by "reading your palm." You agree to it. The fortune teller looks closely at your hand for a minute and then tells you what will happen in your life in the future.

ACTIVITIES

1. *With a partner.* Act out this situation. One of you plays the fortune teller, who will answer questions asked by the other partner. When you have finished, switch roles.

The following are suggestions for questions to ask the fortune teller:

a. How long will I live? Will I be healthy or ill most of my life?

b. Will I marry? (If you are already married, ask: Will I have children?) (If you already have children, ask: Will I have more children?) Will I have grandchildren? How many? Boys or girls? Will I be happy with my family life?

Or Will I stay single? Will I live alone or with other people? Will I be happy being single?

c. How far will I go with my education? What will I study? Will I get a degree? What kind? In what field of study? Will I learn English well? What will I be able to do in English that I can't do now?

d. What kind of work will I do? Will I change jobs often? Will I have my own business or go into a profession? Will I make a lot of money? Will I be happy with my work?

e. Where will I spend most of my life? In this country? Which part? Or back in my native country? Or in some other country?

f. Will I travel? To which countries? Why? With whom?

g. Will there be any disappointments in my life? Are there things that I want to do that I will not be able to do? Are there things that I want to have that I will not be able to have?

h. What will be the happiest and/or the most satisfying part of my life? Will people remember me after I am gone? Who? Why?

i. Ask any other questions that you would like to.

2. *By yourself.* Write out the words of the fortune teller, predicting what will happen to you in your life. Begin this way:

    The fortune teller said, "I will . . ."

3. Tell what the fortune teller said in reported (indirect) speech. Begin this way:

    The fortune teller said that I would . . .

    You may use the following examples to help in writing Activity 3.

Direct Speech	Indirect Speech
He said, "You will live to be 100."	He said I would live to be 100.
"You will marry soon."	He told me (that) I would marry soon.
"People will remember you for . . ."	He said (that) people would remember me for . . .

A LETTER HOME

ACTIVITY

Write a letter about yourself to a friend or relative. Use the following questions as a guide:

a. Ask your correspondent how he/she is feeling. Tell him/her how you are feeling.

b. What are you doing right now (in addition to writing this letter)? Are you eating or drinking anything? What are the other people in your home or class doing right now? Is anything happening outside or in the room at this moment?

c. Where are you living now? Whom are you living with? Are you working? Where? What kind of work are you doing? Are you going to school this year? Where? What are you studying? What courses are you taking this semester?

d. What are you doing after class or this evening? Where are you having dinner tonight or tomorrow night? What are you having? Are you having anyone over for dinner this week? What are you serving?

e. Are you buying or getting something new soon (clothing, a VCR, a stereo, a car, a new apartment or home)? Are you starting anything new? What? When? What are you planning to do in the future?

f. Ask your correspondent to write to you soon. Your letter should look like this:

                                                    Your address
                                                    Today's date

Dear_____,
        How are you feeling? I _____.
I _____.
_____
_____
_____.

                                        Yours truly,
                                        (Sign your name)

(You may also close a friendly letter with Sincerely,/Your friend,/With love,/Affectionately,/All my love,/Love,.)

THE FIRE

ACTIVITIES

1. *With a partner, or in a group.* Describe a fire that you saw.

2. *By yourself.* Write about what you saw. You may use any details you wish in your writing.

or *With a partner.* You and your partner decide together what details you want to include in your story. Both of you write exactly the same thing on your papers. When you have finished, check each other's papers to make sure you have written the same thing and that there are no errors.

Recently there was a fire in your neighborhood. You and your friend watched the fire and saw everything that happened.

Use the following questions to guide you in your selection and organization of details.

a. Where was the fire? In your house? Across the street? In another part of town? In a store? In a vacant building? In your best friend's home? When did the fire occur? At what time did the fire start? Where were you when the fire started?

b. What was the fire caused by? A child playing with matches? A faulty electrical circuit? Food left to burn on the stove? Was the fire accidental? Or was it set by an arsonist?

c. Who reported the fire? How did this person report the fire? By phone? By pulling the alarm at the corner? By running to the fire house? By stopping a passing police car? How many engines and fire fighters responded to the alarm? How long did it take for the fire engines to arrive at the fire? What did you and your friend do when you heard the engines coming?

d. What did the fire fighters do when they first arrived? Did they locate the fire right away? What did they do to put out the fire? Did they use fire hoses? ladders? axes? Did they have to rescue someone trapped in the building?

e. How long did it take them to put out the fire? How much damage did the fire do? Did it burn the entire building? Only one floor? Did the fire spread to other buildings? Were any people injured? Were any families left homeless?

f. What did you and your friend do after the fire fighters left?

THE ROBBERY

ACTIVITIES

1. *With a partner, or in a group.* Describe a robbery that you witnessed or heard about.

2. *By yourself.* Write about a robbery that occurred recently. You may use any details you wish in writing your story.

or *With a partner.* You and your partner decide together what details you want to include in your story. Each of you writes the story on your own papers. When you have finished, exchange papers and help each other correct any errors that you find.

Recently there was a robbery in your neighborhood. You witnessed it or heard about it.

Use the following questions to guide you in your selection and organization of details.

a. Where was the robbery? In a home? In a small grocery store? In a bank? In a large clothing store? What is the name of the place that was robbed? Where is it located? When did the robbery occur? At what time?

b. How many robbers were there? What sex were they? How old were they? Were they tall or short? What were they wearing? What kind of weapons, if any, were they carrying?

c. What did the robbers tell the victim(s) to do? What did the robbers take? Money? Jewelry? Clothing? Nothing? What did the robbers do to the victim(s) before they left? Was anyone injured?

d. What did the victim(s) do after the robbers left? Did the police come? What did the police do? Chase the robbers? Question the victim(s)? Nothing? Were the robbers caught?

e. How did the victim(s) feel about the robbery? Calm? Angry? Afraid? What will they do in the future? Carry a gun? Get a job in a safer neighborhood? Move to a different city? Buy a watchdog?

THE WEDDING

ACTIVITIES

1. *With a partner, or in a group.* Describe a wedding that you attended recently.

2. *By yourself.* Write about a wedding that you attended recently. You may use any details you wish in your writing.

   With a partner. You and your partner decide together what details you want to include in your story. Each of you writes the story on your own papers. When you have finished, exchange papers and help each other correct any errors that you find.

   Next week, David Bloomfield and Maria Redfern are getting married. You are close friends with one or both of them. Write about them, their wedding, and their plans.

   Use the following questions to guide you in your selection and organization of details.

a. *The wedding.* Time? Place? Will it be a religious ceremony or a civil ceremony? Who and how many will be in the bridal party? Dress? Reception? Number of guests?

b. *Description of the bride.* Physical appearance? Age? Much older or younger than the groom? Married before? Any children? Working? What kind of work? Student? What is she studying? Reason for wanting to get married? Love? Money? Desire to escape from her parents? Looking for a substitute father? Other?

c. *Description of the groom.* Physical appearance? Age? Much older or younger than the bride? Married before? Any children? Working? What kind of work? Student? What is he studying? Reason for wanting to get married? Love? Money? Desire to escape from his parents? Looking for a substitute mother? Other?

d. *Reaction of the bride's or groom's parents to the wedding.* Happy? Upset with the idea of losing their daughter/son? Do they like the groom/bride? Why or why not? Promised to give the couple something? What? Money? A house? Furniture? Threatened to do something if their child marries? What? Disinherit her/him? Refuse to see her/him again?

e. *Plans.* Honeymoon? Where? How long? Where will they live? In a large house? In a small apartment? With the bride's/groom's parents? Are they planning to raise a family?

A LECTURE

Pretend that you returned to your native country after spending some time in the United States. You are asked to lecture to a group of university students about life in the U.S. As you prepare the lecture, think about the kinds of questions that students in your country might ask, and try to answer them.

ACTIVITIES

1. *With a partner or in a group.* Compare your answers to some of the questions below.

2. *By yourself.* Write out in English the lecture that you would give.

3. Write about one aspect of American life, such as the rights of women, comparing it to the situation in your native country.

    In parts of the United States that you have lived in or visited:

a. Are most Americans friendly to foreigners? Do they usually try to help? Are they courteous in stores and on trains and busses? Do many Americans speak your native language? Do they try to understand if you have difficulty with English? Is it easy to make friends with Americans?

b. Are most Americans rich? Do most of them have cars? Do most of them have refrigerators, washing machines, dishwashers, VCRs? Are most of them generous?

c. How do most students dress? What do they wear to school? to parties? to weddings?

d. Is it easy to get a job in the United States? What kinds of jobs can you get if you don't speak much English?

e. Is it easy to get into school? Is it expensive? How is school in the U.S. different from school in your native country? Do the teachers treat you differently? Is the work easier or more difficult? Is it difficult if you don't know much English? Can you learn English in school?

f. Is there much crime in the United States? What kind? Do many Americans have guns? Is life in America the same as shown on television and in films?

g. How are women treated? Can they get a good education? Can they get good jobs? Can they go out alone to parties, to bars, to the movies?

h. When do most Americans eat meals? Which foods and beverages do many of them like? What kind of entertainment and activities do they like?

i. Are there any other questions someone might ask you? Is there anything else important that you should say about the United States?

STORY COMPLETION

THE LOTTERY

I sat in front of my television set, as I had done a hundred times before, watching the numbered balls spinning around in the drum. But this week the jackpot was unusually large—$10 million—and I knew there were a million people like me watching and hoping.

The first ball was drawn out of the drum and rolled to a stop. "Number 8," said the announcer. That was one of my numbers. I played the same six numbers every week.

"Number 12," said the announcer. I had two numbers now, but several times before I'd had the first two numbers and never won.

The next ball was number 44, my lucky number. I had three numbers, and my heart began to beat faster. I knew I had a good chance of winning one of the smaller prizes, but could I win the $10 million?

"Number 28," said the announcer. I jumped up from the chair. Four numbers in a row! Could it be happening? I prayed for a moment; then I shouted. I felt the blood rushing to my head.

"Number 27." I had five numbers! I needed only one more. I needed number 6. "Number 6, number 6. Come on number 6," I yelled at the television set. Was it possible? Would I be rich? Would I be able to live the life I had dreamed about?

The sixth ball dropped, and as it rolled briefly to its resting place beside the others I tried to make out the number. I couldn't be sure. It looked like a 6—or was it a 9? That moment was an eternity. Then the announcer spoke.

ACTIVITIES

1. *By yourself.* Complete the story. Did you win or lose? Describe how you felt. What was the first thing you did?

2. *With your partner or your group.* Talk about lotteries. Do you think lotteries are a good idea? Does your state or country have one? Do you play? Do you expect to win? Have you ever won anything? If you won a fortune, what would you do with the money?

3. *Interview.* Pretend that your partner won the lottery and you are interviewing him/her. Ask what he/she plans to do with the money. Together, write down the questions and answers on one sheet of paper. Then switch roles and do the same thing.

4. *By yourself.* Pretend that it is six months since you won the money. Write a letter to a friend telling him or her what you are doing right now.

OUT OF GAS

Bill Richardson, an American, was on vacation in a beautiful country. He was driving alone along a narrow mountain road trying to get to Canstaadt, an isolated mountain village. It was dusk, growing dark and cold, and Bill was getting scared. He knew that it was dangerous in the mountains, especially at night. Several people had disappeared in these mountains during the past couple of weeks and no one could find them. At that moment the car slowed down and then stopped. Bill looked at the fuel gauge. "Oh, no!" he groaned. The car was out of gas. He got out of the car and looked around. He couldn't see anyone or anything. He sat down at the side of the road to think.

Suddenly, he heard a noise.

ACTIVITY

By yourself, or with a partner. Finish writing this story.

AN UNFORGETTABLE NIGHT

The night started out so well for us. Bill picked me up on time and we were off to a night of dancing at the Casa Blanca. We had been looking forward to this night for two weeks, ever since we heard that Johnny Ventura and his orchestra were going to play.

Bill parked around the corner from the club and we went in. We were early on purpose so that we could get a table near the dance floor and the orchestra. A waiter brought us a bottle of White Label and we sat sipping our drinks. Gradually the club began to fill with other couples: women in ruffled gowns or fancy blouses with brightly colored pants; men in jacket and tie or open-necked shirts and vests. Everyone looked beautiful. They sat or stood in groups, talking excitedly while waiting for their favorite orchestra to appear.

Finally, Johnny and his group arrived. They quickly set up on the stage, warmed up, and were ready to play. As they began their first number—a merengue, of course—Bill and I jumped up to dance. We were happy in each other's arms, dancing to the swirling rhythms of the orchestra. We didn't sit down again until they had finished the first set. While they took a break, Bill and I sat talking about our plans. We had become engaged a month before and were planning to get married in June. We had some problems to consider, but we were confident that we could solve them. We were happy knowing that we loved each other and would soon be starting our life together.

The music started again and we danced the second set. When the orchestra took another break, I went to the ladies room. It took a few minutes because the room was crowded. When I left the ladies room, I saw someone else at our table. Bill was sitting where I had left him, but a woman I had never seen before was standing next to him. She was leaning over him, and her long, shiny, black hair was brushing against his cheek. He was holding her hand and looking into her eyes. Suddenly she leaned over even further and kissed him. He didn't pull his lips away.

I stood still for a moment, watching them. Then slowly I walked over to the table.

ACTIVITIES

1. *With your partner or group.* Discuss this story. Who was the other woman? What would you do if you were the woman telling the story? What would you do if you were Bill?

2. *By yourself.* Write the ending to the story.

   Or, pretend that you are Bill and finish the story.

   You may use the following examples to help in writing the ending to the story.

Direct Speech	**Indirect Speech**
"I will call."	I said I would call.
I asked Bill, "Who is she?"	I asked Bill who she was.
"What is she doing here?" I asked him.	I asked him what she was doing there.
He said, "She is . . ."	He said (that) she was . . .
"It's nothing," he replied.	He replied that it was nothing.
He said, "I was drunk."	He said (that) he had been drunk.
I said to Bill, "I want . . ."	I told Bill that I wanted . . .
"I think . . . ," I told him.	I told him (that) I thought . . .

3. Write about what you would have done if you had been the woman in the situation. Begin this way:

   If I had been the woman I would have . . .

BOB

Bob liked Barcelona. He frequently walked up and down the Ramblas, looking at the people. He often stopped to browse at the magazine stands or to watch the vendors selling handicrafts and lottery tickets and birds and rabbits. Then he liked to sit down at one of the cafés, have a drink, and watch the people again. Some evenings he wandered through the old part of the city, stopping in small, noisy bars for a glass of wine and some snacks they called *tapas,* like the sausage called *chorizo,* which they covered in a clear, flavored brandy and set on fire— *al diablo*—before eating.

Although he didn't speak Spanish, within a month Bob felt very much at home. He met a lot of English-speaking people who were friendly and helpful. One helped him find a job, another an apartment. He learned enough Spanish words so that he could get the things he needed in shops and order what he wanted in restaurants. But most of the time, the only language he needed was English. He spoke to his friends in English. He read English newspapers and listened to broadcasts from England on his short-wave radio to find out what was happening in the world. He even found some English-language films to see. And on his job teaching English to bank clerks every morning, he didn't have to speak the language of his students. Most of the time he didn't try. It was certainly much easier to speak your own language than to speak another one, letting people know that you were a foreigner and taking the risk of having them laugh at you.

But there was a lot missing. He couldn't understand television or go to the theater, and he felt isolated from the things that were going on in this city and country he was living in. He also knew that he could not get a good full-time job and make enough money to live comfortably without being able to speak and read and write Spanish very well. He knew that it would be difficult to do, but if he didn't try, he would have to go back to the United States, where he had no job, no family, and few friends. And he didn't want to do that.

ACTIVITIES

1. *Retelling.* Tell Bob's story to a partner or other members of the class.

2. *With your partner or group.* Discuss the following questions.

   a. What two choices did Bob have?

   b. What did he want to do? Why?

   c. Why did he prefer life in Barcelona to life in a big city in the United States?

   d. Why was it difficult for him to learn Spanish?

   e. What did he have to do (and what did he have to stop doing) if he wanted to learn Spanish well?

   f. Try to describe Bob. How old was he? What kind of education did he have? Which details in the story helped you to answer these questions?

   g. What did Bob enjoy doing?

   h. What decision do you think he made? Why?

3. *By yourself.* In writing, complete Bob's story. Tell what he did and how he did it. Be specific—give details.

GRACE'S DILEMMA

Grace is 22 years old. She has been living in the United States for four years. She came to the U.S. to be a doctor. She is in her third year at a large university, where she is studying premed. She likes college very much and is doing well in her studies. Recently, her counselor told her that she has a good chance for a four-year scholarship to study medicine. Grace feels that she will be able to begin studying medicine soon. She is involved in a meaningful relationship with a young man named Dan. Everything is going well in her life and she feels very happy.

Yesterday she received a letter from her mother in Peru. This is what the letter said:

Dear Grace,

It is very difficult for me to write this letter to you because I know that you are happy in the United States and are studying successfully at the university. But I have to tell you that I am getting sick. I am old now and the doctors have told me that I will not get better. I need someone to take care of me. Please, Grace, come home and stay with your mother. I need you. I am asking you and not your brother because you know that he is married and has children. Write to me right away and let me know that you are coming.

Love,
Your Mother

ACTIVITIES

1. *Retelling.* Tell Grace's story to a partner or other members of the class.

2. *With your partner or group.* Discuss the following questions.

   a. What did Grace decide to do?
   b. If she decided to go back to Peru, what happened to her career and her relationship with Dan?
   c. If she decided to stay in the United States, what happened to her mother?
   d. Did she decide right away? Did she talk to someone first?

3. *By yourself.* In writing, complete Grace's story. Tell what she did and how and why she did it. Be specific—give details.

UNFINISHED STORY

Roselyn kissed Larry once more. He was so warm and she felt so secure in his arms. She didn't want to leave this tender and loving man, but it was time to go. Her children would be home soon from school. Roselyn and Larry made plans to see each other again in a few days. Then Roselyn left.

While she waited for a cab outside Larry's apartment, she thought about how happy she was. She hadn't felt so alive in years. Larry was good for her. He made her feel loved and wanted. He understood her needs and feelings. They had grown very close, even though they had known each other only a short time.

Roselyn got home just a few minutes before her son and daughter. Her children were a big part of her life. She loved them dearly. She worried about them constantly because she didn't want anything bad to happen to them. Until recently, they had been the only love in her life. She and her husband Phil had stopped loving each other years ago. They only continued living together because of the children. But now Larry was in her life. She thought about how happy she and Larry and the children would be together.

It was time to make a decision. If she got a divorce, she would be free to be with Larry. But she might lose the children. Her husband loved them very much also. If Roselyn tried to get a divorce, Phil would fight hard to get custody of the children. Roselyn loved and needed Larry very much, but she loved and needed her children, too, and she didn't want to live without them.

Roselyn knew that she had to make a decision before she saw Larry again in a few days.

ACTIVITIES

1. *Retelling*. Tell Roselyn's story to your partner or group. Try to answer any questions that they ask.

2. *With your partner or group*. Discuss the story. What possible decisions could Roselyn make? How might Phil and Larry react to each decision? How might her children react? If you were Roselyn's friend, what would you advise her to do?

3. *By yourself*. Write an ending to this story in which Roselyn followed your advice. Or write an ending in which she did not follow your advice. In either case, tell what happened to all the people involved. Be specific—give details.

MODEL COMPOSITIONS

INTERVIEW WITH KENNETH

My classmate's name is Kenneth Wong. He comes from Asia. He has been in this country for only one year. He is single and lives with his aunt and uncle. His parents and brothers and sisters are in Hong Kong. He came to this country to finish his education. He is studying to be an electrical engineer.

Kenneth has many interests besides school. He enjoys disco music and he often goes dancing with friends. He also likes photography. He showed me some pictures that he took. They were excellent.

Kenneth says that he likes his school and that he likes this country. He wants to stay here, become a citizen, and bring his family here.

ACTIVITIES

1. Interview a classmate. You may ask the questions below and other questions you can think of. Write the answers.

2. Tell a group or the class about the person you interviewed. Give that person a chance to correct any errors that you make. Try to answer any questions that the students ask.

3. Use the information to write a composition about your classmate. The composition about Kenneth can serve as a model for you.

Here are some questions and answers that can be used in the interview:

QUESTIONS	ANSWERS
Where are you from?	I'm from . . .
	I come from . . .
Who(m) do you live with?	I live with . . .
	I live alone/by myself.
How old are you?	I am _____ years old.
How long have you lived/been here?	I've lived/been here for a long time/a year/ since 1986.
Where is your family?	My family is in . . .
What do you plan to do in the future?	I plan to . . .
Why did you come to the United States?	I came to the U.S. because . . .
When do you expect to graduate?	I expect to graduate in . . .

A FAVORITE DISH

My father grew up in Romania, and one of his special memories was of the eggplant salad that his mother used to prepare. My father used to make it in our home, but he said it never tasted quite the same as it did when his mother made it. She used to take a freshly picked eggplant and cook it on top of a woodburning stove until it was slightly burned on the outside and soft on the inside. My father said his mouth used to water when he smelled the burnt aroma of that lovely fresh eggplant, and that he could hardly wait for dinner time to taste the sharp, smoky flavor. My father made it for us only on holidays, cooking the eggplant on top of our gas stove, and I can remember when I was a child looking forward to tasting that delicious dish, just as my father had when he was a child.

PAPA MARCO'S EGGPLANT SALAD

Select a firm eggplant, purple in color, weighing about $1\frac{1}{4}$ pounds. Wash it and put it directly on top of an oven burner over a very low flame. As it starts to burn, turn it so that every part of the vegetable is blackened and softened by the flame. This should take about 45 minutes. While the eggplant is cooking, chop a small onion into small pieces and sauté it in oil in a frying pan until it is light brown. When the eggplant is done, remove it to a dish and let it cool. Then peel off the skin and put the vegetable into a bowl. Add two tablespoons of vegetable oil, one tablespoon of apple cider vinegar, $\frac{1}{4}$ teaspoon of salt, a sprinkling of red pepper, and the sautéed onions. Mash the mixture with a fork until it is smooth. Serve on a large platter on a base of lettuce leaves. Garnish with sliced tomatoes, radishes, and green olives.

The soft, flat Middle Eastern bread called pita is excellent with this dish and can be used to scoop up the eggplant salad like a dip. I prefer to drink beer with this, but a chilled, very dry Greek or Romanian wine is also a good accompaniment.

ACTIVITIES

1. Think about one of your favorite dishes from childhood. Try to remember all the ingredients that go into it and how it is prepared. Then describe the recipe to a partner, giving all the details necessary. Your partner will write the recipe and ask you questions about it. After your partner finishes writing the recipe, check it to make sure it is accurate and that there are no errors in grammar or spelling.

    When this is completed, your partner will describe a recipe to you, and you will write it.

2. Write an introduction about your favorite dish that tells why it is your favorite. Answer some of the following questions in your introduction:

    a. Who prepared it for you?

    b. When did you first eat it? As a child? With someone special when you were older?

    c. Where did you usually eat this dish?

MY LIFE

I was born in Athens, Greece, on January 11, 1965. My father was a businessman and my mother stayed home and took care of our house and family. I have four brothers and sisters; two sisters and a brother are older than I am and one brother is younger. When I was a child, my friends and I went everywhere we wanted, and my younger brother tagged along after me. We roamed the streets and climbed the hills, played soccer and gambled with cards and dice, and sometimes stole things from stores. My father used to punish me for doing some of these things.

From the ages of six to twelve I went to school in Athens, but I wasn't a very good student. In 1975, my family left Greece and came to this country. It was difficult for me at first because I didn't have any friends and I didn't understand the language, but I went to high school and made friends and learned a lot.

When I finished high school I went to work for my father. I also met a lovely Greek girl named Urania and we got married in June 1985. Now we have a one-year-old boy named Alexander. We live in a neighborhood where there are many Greek people and we keep a lot of the same customs we had in the old country. We eat many of the same foods and we celebrate the holidays in similar ways. I especially like the evening candle procession around the church at Easter.

Now that I have a family to take care of, I am much more serious about life than I used to be, and I have decided to return to school to get a degree and to improve my knowledge of English. I would like to be a professional some day.

ACTIVITIES

1. Tell your partner or group the major events and aspects of the author's life. What is the most important way he has changed?

2. Think about the most important events and aspects of your life so far: for example, where and when you were born; your parents and brothers and sisters; your schooling; important changes in your life; marriage; children. Also think about some specific incidents from your childhood or more recently that you might like to describe and the most important way you have changed in recent years. Then write about yourself.

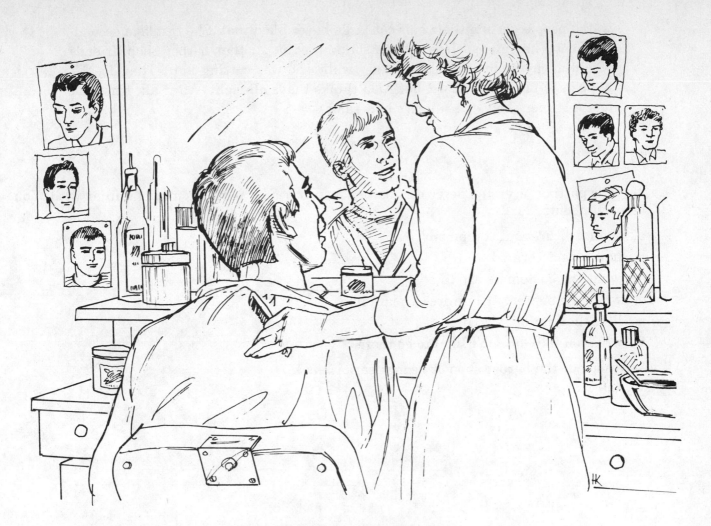

THE BARBER SHOP

You have to climb a long flight of dimly lit stairs to get to Aida and Caroline's hairstyling salon. But its big glass windows face out onto Broadway and the shop is light and pleasant. If you have an appointment, there is usually only a short wait.

First, Aida shampoos your hair. She puts a plastic covering over you and leans your head backward into a sink. She gives the hair two separate washes and then wraps a towel around your head to dry it. Next she seats you in the barber's chair and with scissors and comb spends almost an hour cutting your hair. There is a mirror in front of the chair with a shelf holding different kinds of hair dressings, each a different color and each in a different kind of bottle. The sinks and coat rack are in back of you and Caroline's chair is on the right. There are pictures of good-looking men with different hair styles around the mirror and on the wall to your left. As Aida cuts your hair she talks about herself and her family, and often about God. But you don't have to listen; she usually doesn't expect a response. If you have a beard, she will trim it for you before she's done. She is very careful and your hair always looks good when she's finished.

Aida likes having her shop on the second floor because it gives her customers privacy. In most barber shops you can look through the big glass windows and watch people getting their hair cut. Aida never liked that. She thinks a second-floor shop has more "class." When she worked in another barber shop, friends would always come in to talk to her while she was cutting hair. That doesn't happen so much any more, but Aida thinks that's all right. After all, this isn't just a barber shop—it's a men's hair salon.

ACTIVITIES

1. To your partner or group, describe a barber shop or beauty parlor you are familiar with. You can tell about:

   a. the furniture and equipment
   b. how it is decorated
   c. what the customers are like
   d what the barbers or hairdressers are like
   e. how they cut or style hair
   f. why you like (or don't like) to go there

2. Write about the barber shop or beauty parlor.

ANECDOTE

Our professor of comparative religion seemed well suited to teach his subject. He looked like a biblical prophet with his ragged gray beard and serious face, and he always gave us difficult assignments.

It was not surprising, then, that on the day of our final examination we came into the classroom expecting the worst. As if reflecting our fears that day, the sky was dark and a storm threatened.

Right on time, the professor arrived and without even greeting us he began reading aloud his first question in a deep voice. Our fears had been justified. Not daring to make a sound, we could only wait quietly in our seats and listen to the endless question. It covered the entire semester's work, asking for detailed comparisons of the major religions and requiring specific information from the textbook and classroom notes.

He had barely finished reading when an angry sound of thunder came rumbling down from the overcast sky, ending in a tremendous roar that shook the room and rattled the windows. Without hesitating, our professor looked angrily upward, and shaking his finger at the ceiling overhead, thundered back, "And that's only the first question."

ACTIVITIES

1. Tell your partner or group about an amusing incident that you or someone you know experienced.

2. Write the anecdote.

A LETTER OF COMPLAINT

888 Oakhurst Circle
Sarasota, FL 34232
(813) 777-1212
July 21, 1988

J.K.L. Auto Repair, Inc.
600 Main Street
Sarasota, FL 34231

Dear J.K.L.:

On March 17th of this year I used your towing service, as recommended by the Peninsula Automobile Club, and was towed to your repair shop. You replaced a number of parts, including an alternator ($66.77) and a voltage regulator ($29.46). The labor charge for replacing these parts and installing two alternator belts was $52.80. (See copy of invoice attached.) The odometer reading at the time of repair was 49,256 miles.

On July 7th, less than four months after this repair, with an odometer reading of 50,509 miles, the battery went dead. A check of the car by my regular mechanic found the alternator not functioning because of overcharging by a faulty regulator. Both of these parts had to be replaced. (See second invoice attached.)

Although you guarantee your electrical parts for only thirty days, it seems unreasonable to me to have to replace these parts in less than four months, after only 1,250 miles of driving. I am therefore asking for a partial refund of the cost of the faulty parts and labor as follows:

90% of $66.77 (alternator)	$60.09
90% of 29.46 (voltage regulator)	26.51
50% of 52.80 (labor)	26.40
5% tax	5.65
for a total of	$118.65

If you would like to discuss this matter further, please contact me.

Yours truly,

cc: Peninsula Automobile Club

ACTIVITIES

1. Tell your partner or group about a complaint you have regarding unsatisfactory goods or services. Get suggestions about whom to write to and what to ask for.

2. Write a letter of complaint to an individual, a company, or a government agency explaining in detail the situation you are unhappy about. Tell them specifically what you would like done about the situation.

DIALOGUES

LUISA RODRIGUEZ AND HER MOTHER

Mrs. Rodriguez came here from an island country in the Caribbean. Even though she's been here for fifteen years, she still holds onto the ideas and customs of her native country. Her children follow the traditional custom of asking for her blessing whenever they leave the house. She doesn't allow her teenage daughter, Luisa, to go out alone. When Luisa comes home from school, she has to stay in the house. She isn't allowed to go to parties on the weekends or to go out with boys, even though she's seventeen years old. Mrs. Rodriguez says she has to wait until she graduates from high school. She loves her daughter very much, but she is strict with her because she believes that is the best way to raise her children.

Luisa wasn't born here but she came here when she was a child. Since the third grade she's gone to American schools and has had American friends. Her friends stay outside on the street after school. They go to parties and on dates. Luisa wants to be with them and do what they do. Recently she became attracted to Tony, a boy in the same class at school. Tony has asked her to go out with him and she wants to accept. Luisa loves her mother and respects her ways, but she really would like her mother to give her more freedom. She knows that she's going to have a hard time convincing her mother.

Last night after her brothers and sisters had gone to bed, Luisa talked with her mother about Tony, her desire to go out with him, and her desire to have more freedom like her friends have.

ACTIVITIES

1. *Retelling.* After you have read about Luisa Rodriguez and her mother, tell the story to your partner or group in your own words.

2. *Role playing*. You and your partner play the roles of Luisa and her mother. Have a conversation and say to each other the things that Luisa and her mother would say. To help you decide what they would say to each other, remember that:

MRS. RODRIGUEZ
- loves her daughter.
- is raising her in a traditional way.
- wants Luisa to wait until she graduates from high school before she starts going out with boys.

LUISA
- loves her mother.
- wants to be more like her American friends.
- likes Tony and wants to go out with him.

3. *Dialogue writing*. In the form of a dialogue, write the conversation that you think Luisa had with her mother. You and your partner will write this dialogue together. Write the dialogue like this:

LUISA: Mom, I want to talk to you about something important.

MOTHER: O.K., Luisa, what is it?

LUISA: _____.

MOTHER: _____.

   Remember that both you and your partner are responsible for sharing the ideas and the writing of this dialogue. Be sure to write both Luisa's sentences and her mother's sentences on one piece of paper so that the complete dialogue will be together.

4. Pretend that you are Luisa's older brother. You are responsible for her welfare because your mother had to return to her native country. With another member of the class, write out the conversation that you and Luisa would have about this situation.

ANNA AND MARTIN

Anna and Martin are married and have been living in the United States for ten years. Martin drives a delivery truck and earns enough money to pay the rent on their four-room apartment and to buy enough food and clothing for them and their two young children, a boy and a girl. But he also likes to go out a couple of nights a week to drink and play cards, or to go to a ball game with his friends. Anna doesn't mind his going out, but there is no money left over for her to do the things that she would like to do. She would also like to save money to buy a house and some special things for the children. She has decided that she would like to go to work.

She hasn't discussed this with Martin yet, but she thinks he would not approve. First of all, in their native country it is not as common for women to work as it is in the United States. Secondly, she knows that Martin is very proud and would not like the idea of his wife working. He thinks a wife should stay home and take care of her own home and family. She thinks there are enough good reasons for her to go to work, and she decides to discuss the situation with Martin. One night, after the children are asleep, she brings up the matter.

ACTIVITIES

1. *Retelling*. After you have read about Anna and Martin, tell the story to your partner or group in your own words.

2. *Role playing*. You and your partner play the roles of Anna and Martin. Have a conversation and say to each other the things that Anna and Martin would say. To help you decide what they would say to each other, remember that:

ANNA

- loves and respects her husband and was brought up to think that "a woman's place is in the home," but they need the money, and, besides, this is modern America and many women work.
- would like money of her own to spend as she pleases without having to ask for it or to give explanations.
- doesn't have enough to keep her occupied all day long; she gets bored.
- feels there is something unfair about the marriage.

MARTIN

- wouldn't like the idea of his wife contributing to support the family and having money of her own to spend any way she wants.
- came to America to have a better life, not so his wife would have to work.
- likes to know that his children are taken care of when they get home from school.

3. *Dialogue writing*. In the form of a dialogue, write the conversation that you think Anna had with Martin. You and your partner will write this dialogue together. Write the dialogue like this:

ANNA: _____.

MARTIN: _____.

Remember that both you and your partner are responsible for sharing the ideas and the writing of this dialogue. Be sure to write both Anna's sentences and Martin's sentences on one piece of paper so that the complete dialogue will be together.

TERRY HARRIS AND HIS FATHER

Mr. Harris, a wealthy, well-known lawyer, is paying for his son's education. He has plans for his son, Terry. He wants him to become a successful lawyer like himself. He dreams that Terry will be a partner in his law firm, will live in a mansion in an exclusive suburb, and will marry a beautiful, educated woman from a "good family."

Twenty-year-old Terry has other ideas. He's sick of college. He has decided that a career in law is just not for him. He wants to drop out of college at the end of the semester. Terry is also in love with Nancy, a waitress who works in a coffee shop near the campus. He wants to marry her.

Terry went home last weekend to talk to his father about his plans.

ACTIVITIES

1. *Retelling*. Explain to your partner or group the conflict between Terry and his father.

2. *Role playing*. You and your partner play the roles of Terry and his father. Have a conversation and say to each other the things that you think they would say.

3. *Dialogue writing*. In the form of a dialogue, write the conversation that you think Terry had with his father. You and your partner will write this dialogue together.

JOE AND IDA

Joe and Ida are married. They have been living in the United States for five years. They came to the U.S. together from their native country of _____, where they were married twelve years ago. They have two children—Leo, who is ten years old, and Sara, who is four.

Ida wants to go back to _____, but Joe does not. Ida says it would be better for the children. They would have nicer friends, not get into trouble, and get a better education. There is less crime in _____, the weather is more pleasant, and it is cheaper and easier to live there.

Joe says that he can earn a much better living in the United States. All his friends are here now. The children will be better off because they will be able to get a college education and eventually get good jobs. He calls the United States "the land of opportunity."

One evening, Joe and Ida discuss this matter.

ACTIVITIES

1. *Retelling.* Explain to your partner or group the conflict between Joe and Ida.

2. *Role playing.* You and your partner play the roles of Joe and Ida. Have a conversation and say to each other the things that you think they would say.

3. *Dialogue writing.* In the form of a dialogue, write the conversation that you think Joe had with Ida. You and your partner will write this dialogue together.

JOHN AND CYNTHIA BARTON

John is fed up. He can't take any more of it. Nora, his mother-in-law, has got to go! When his wife, Cynthia, first suggested that her mother come to live with them for a while, John thought it was a good idea. But now that she's been living in his house for five months? Forget it! John wishes his mother-in-law would go to the moon. She's too nosy. She has to know everything that's going on. When he and Cynthia have a disagreement over something, his mother-in-law has to butt in with her opinion. It's impossible to have any privacy. She's costing John money, too. She makes frequent calls to friends back in Chicago and talks with them for hours. His monthly phone bills are enormous. And if all this wasn't enough, John knows that Nora doesn't like him. She feels that her daughter could've found a better husband. Because of all this, John wants his mother-in-law out.

Cynthia is glad that her mother's living with them. Nora is a big help with the children. Cynthia leaves the children with her when she has to go out. The children like their grandma because she always has candy or cookies for them. Cynthia also appreciates her company. Sometimes John works overtime and gets home late. On those nights Cynthia doesn't have to wait up alone. Nora also helps with the housework and the cooking. Cynthia's life would be much more difficult if her mother wasn't there.

Tonight when John comes from work, he's going to talk to Cynthia about his mother-in-law.

ACTIVITIES

1. *Retelling.* Using your own words, tell the story again to your partner or group.

2. *Role playing.* You and your partner play the roles of John and Cynthia. Have a conversation and say to each other the things that you think they would say.

3. *Dialogue writing.* In the form of a dialogue, write the conversation that you think John and Cynthia will have tonight. You and your partner write this dialogue together.

STEVE AND ELIZABETH

Elizabeth has been going with Steve for almost a year and the relationship has become serious. She has the feeling that Steve's about to ask her to marry him. Elizabeth feels that she's not ready to get married. She is in her second year of college and she wants to finish her education and begin her career before she thinks about marriage and a family. Besides, she is only nineteen and Steve is her first real boyfriend. Even though she's in love with him, she's not sure he's the man she wants to spend the rest of her life with.

Steve is 26. He is very much in love with Elizabeth. He's had other girl-friends. Now, after going out with Elizabeth for a year, he knows he's found the right woman to be his wife and the mother of his children. He's crazy about her and wants to be married to her for the rest of his life.

This Saturday night, while out on a very special date, Steve plans to propose to Elizabeth.

ACTIVITIES

1. *Retelling.* Using your own words, explain to your partner or group how Elizabeth feels. Explain how Steve feels.

2. *Role playing.* You and your partner play the roles of Steve and Elizabeth. Have a conversation and say to each other the things that you think they would say.

3. *Dialogue writing.* In the form of a dialogue, write the conversation that you think Steve and Elizabeth will have on Saturday night. You and your partner will write this dialogue together.

READ AND WRITE

MY GRANDMA'S HOUSE

When I came home from school each day as a child, I grabbed a handful of cookies or a box of raisins to eat and ran up to my grandma's house. Her house was a half mile from where I lived.

It was an old house built on a hill. The outside was painted yellow and green. It was difficult to see from the road because it was surrounded by pine trees. To reach the house you had to walk up a long driveway. When I went there in the spring or summer, Grandma was always working in her garden so I didn't bother to go inside. Instead I climbed the stone steps in back of the house and walked along the path until I found her bent over her plants. Grandma was always glad to see me because I was her favorite grandchild and also because I helped her do the things that were important to her. She was getting old, so each spring I dug the garden for her and helped her plant. We planted rows and rows of tomatoes, corn, green peppers, string beans, radishes, and many other kinds of vegetables.

Each day after we finished working in the garden, we went inside the house. It was warm and friendly inside, especially in the kitchen. It was a large kitchen, filled with all the pots, pans, jars, bottles, and other things Grandma needed to bake homemade bread, make noodles for soup, and preserve some of the vegetables that came from the garden. While I sat at the kitchen table and watched, Grandma cooked dinner for my aunt and uncle, who still lived with her. She was a great cook. I can never forget the enormous meals she prepared for the entire family on holidays.

On some days when I got tired of watching Grandma cook, I picked up a watering can from the floor next to the sink, filled it, and went to the front porch. Grandma kept her plants there because it faced west and had many large windows. She had dozens of plants, some big, some small, all lined up on tables in front of the windows. She loved plants and she taught me to love them, too. She said that plants and flowers were given to us by God to make our lives more beautiful. I watered the plants, giving some a lot of water and others only a little as Grandma had taught me to do.

By the time I returned to the kitchen it was filled with the rich smells of the evening meal. Grandma always gave me a taste of whatever she was cooking.

At 7:00 I had to leave. My mother was waiting for me. I kissed Grandma good-bye, promising to return the next day. Then I walked down the driveway past the tall pine trees and went home.

Grandma died when I was sixteen. My aunt and uncle sold the house and moved away. Now, many years later, the house looks very different. The pine trees are gone and the house is painted blue. There is a small swimming pool in the back where the garden used to be. But whenever I drive by, I always remember the house as it was when Grandma lived there.

ACTIVITIES

1. *Retelling.* Using your own words, tell your partner or group about Grandma's house and why it meant so much to the storyteller.

2. Questions for comprehension:

   a. What did the storyteller do at Grandma's house?
   b. Why did the storyteller like to go there?
   c. What did the storyteller learn from Grandma?
   d. What changes were made to the house after it was sold?

3. Write about a place that had some special meaning for you in the past or has some special meaning for you now.

CHI LIN'S ESCAPE TO FREEDOM

I had to get out. I couldn't stay in my country any longer. A new government had taken control the year before and I hated it. If I stayed, I would join the antigovernment movement, and sooner or later the soldiers would kill me or put me in prison. No, I had to leave. I had to be free.

One night while my parents, brothers, and sisters were sleeping, I got up and left the house. I couldn't tell them where I was going, but it was so painful to leave them without saying good-bye. I walked until daylight, then hid under a tree and slept. When night came again, I got up and continued walking. I travelled this way for three weeks, walking at night and sleeping in caves or under trees during the day. I didn't want to meet anyone who might recognize me. And I was afraid to be seen by the police or soldiers who constantly patrolled the countryside.

I had very little to eat. Sometimes I found some wild fruit, other times some vegetables growing on farmland. Once I killed a chicken. But often I went to sleep hungry. I was becoming weak, but, when I thought of the freedom that waited for me on the other side of the river, I found new strength and I kept going.

Finally, on one very dark night I came to the river. Hearing it before I could see it, I began to run toward it. Suddenly I stopped and didn't move. I heard dogs barking. A patrol was coming along the river bank. Maybe the dogs would sense me. I quickly hid behind some bushes, afraid to move or even breathe. They came closer. I could see three dogs and a half-dozen soldiers. Suddenly the dogs stopped and began sniffing the air. One of the soldiers looked toward the bushes where I was hiding. My heart was pounding. I was sure they would discover me. But then the dogs started moving again and the patrol passed by.

I waited until I couldn't hear the barking of the dogs any longer. Then I waded into the river and swam to the other side.

ACTIVITIES

1. *Retelling.* Using your own words, tell your partner or group about Chi Lin's escape.

2. Questions for comprehension:

   a. Why did Chi Lin decide to leave his country?

   b. Where was Chi Lin going? How long did it take him to get there? Why did he travel at night?

   c. In your opinion, what was Chi Lin's idea of "freedom"? How did he learn about it?

3. Write about your decision (or your parents' decision) to leave your native country. Why was the decision made? Describe your departure. Was it easy or difficult for you to leave? Why?

THE GROCERY STORE

Charlie owns a small grocery store on the corner of Longwood Avenue and Fox Street. Charlie is a nice guy. All the people in the neighborhood know that he is a nice guy. Charlie's store is a little-of-everything-for-everybody kind of store. It carries all kinds of groceries, fresh and canned. It has meat, eggs, and cheese. For the kids there are potato chips, candy, and soda. In the back of the store there is a shelf for school supplies, novelties, and coloring books. Behind the counter Charlie keeps cigarettes, aspirin, Band-aids, and other useful items. Charlie also has a machine to slice meat and cheese for sandwiches.

People run in and out of the store all day long and halfway into the night. Sometimes one person will come in five or six times the same day. Usually it is a little girl who is sent by her mother to buy milk for the baby or more rice for supper or some bananas. Charlie doesn't mind all the business, of course, but if the mother has credit at the store, he has a lot of extra bookkeeping to do.

Charlie opens his store early in the morning. He makes sure that the shelves are filled and then goes outside and carefully sweeps the sidewalk in front. He doesn't want to get a summons from the police. One of his first customers is Mr. Randall. He comes in every morning on his way to work to buy a pack of king-size Marlboros. Mr. Randall is cheerful in the morning. He has a high-paying job and he is proud of it.

A little while later some neighborhood kids come in with quarters to get some breakfast. They usually buy potato chips or soda. Charlie thinks to himself, "No wonder they are so skinny!" When the kids leave for school it is quiet for a while. Then the women begin to come in to get their groceries for the day. They aren't in any hurry. They stand around and talk about what is going on in their building. Charlie turns off his ears to the gossip. One of the women, Carolyn

Maxwell, doesn't listen to the gossip, either. She prefers to talk to Charlie. Charlie thinks that she likes him a lot, but he doesn't want to get involved. She has four kids.

And so the day goes by. When school lets out, the kids play in the street. They run in with dimes and nickels clutched in their sweaty hands. They want soda. Teenage girls look through love stories before deciding which one to buy. Finally Phillip arrives to help him. Phillip is always late but he always has an excuse ready for Charlie. Some of them make Charlie laugh.

Charlie leaves Phillip in charge and goes out to get some supper and a couple of hours rest. At 7:30 he is back. The men are outside now. One or two are fixing their cars. A group is standing on the corner drinking beer and telling jokes. This is the dangerous time of day. It is always possible that someone may start a fight and break his store window. Or maybe someone will try to rob him.

Charlie does a lot of business at night, but he is glad when 11:30 comes and it is time to close up. He shuts the gate, locks it and goes home exhausted. Early tomorrow morning he will be back to take his place again in the life of the people of Longwood Avenue at the corner of Fox Street.

ACTIVITIES

1. *Retelling.* Using your own words, tell your partner or group what you read about Charlie and his store.

2. Questions for comprehension:

   a. What does Charlie do each day when he opens the store?
   b. Who comes to Charlie's store in the morning? In the afternoon? At night?
   c. Why does Charlie leave Phillip in charge of the store in the late afternoon?
   d. How does Charlie feel about keeping his store open at night? What does he worry about?
   e. When it is time to close the store, what does Charlie do? How does he feel?
   f. How do Charlie's customers feel about him?
   g. How does Charlie feel about his customers?
   h. How does Charlie help the neighborhood where his store is located?
   i. Does Charlie like his job? Explain.

3. Write about a storekeeper or about an employee who works in a store in your neighborhood.

UNCLE CARMINE

I remember my Uncle Carmine. He used to come to my house almost every weekend during the fall and winter months of the hunting season. My uncle loved to hunt. He lived in a big city. We lived in the country. He used to keep his 12-gauge shotgun, ammunition, and hunting jacket in a special closet in our basement. He used to arrive early Saturday morning, walking up the hill from the train station carrying two large, round loaves of Italian bread wrapped in brown paper and tied together with a string. I always looked forward to his visits because I loved to eat that bread, but especially because Uncle Carmine always took me hunting with him. I loved to walk by his side always keeping slightly behind him. He insisted on this in case he had to raise his gun to his shoulder quickly and fire. We used to hunt rabbits. When he shot one, he brought it home, skinned it, and let it soak in vinegar until it was ready to be made into rabbit stew. That rabbit stew was delicious. My mother cooked it for us. It tasted especially good to me because I knew that I had helped bring it to the table.

We used to begin the hunt in the woods behind my house. Soon we were climbing hills and walking among the trees. After an hour or two, we came to open fields on the sides of gently rolling hills. We walked along, beating the brush with a stick and hoping to scare a rabbit or perhaps a pheasant. It was usually cold but I never minded. I was too excited by the hope of finding a rabbit. When we felt hungry, we stopped and built a fire. Then Uncle Carmine used to take out several links of fresh, sweet sausage from his pack and place them in a frying pan. Soon they were sizzling on the hot fire. As the aroma reached my nose, I became even more hungry. I could hardly wait. When the sausage was done, we put it between thick slices of my uncle's bread and ate. I can still smell that sausage, hear the crunch of the crusty bread as I bit into it, and taste the hot, juicy sausage.

In the afternoon we continued to hunt. When a rabbit started running in front of us, Uncle Carmine aimed at its hind legs and pulled the trigger. Once in a while he missed, but most of the time he didn't. We ran up to the rabbit quickly. Uncle Carmine picked it up. If it was still alive, he banged its head against a rock so that it would die quickly and not suffer. Then he put it in the big pocket in the back of his hunting jacket.

In the late afternoon when it was beginning to get dark, we headed back home. Sometimes we came back with two or three rabbits. Sometimes we came back empty-handed. But it didn't matter to me. The excitement for me was being out all day miles away from home walking with my uncle and his big gun. Even though I was much too small to carry a gun, I felt big and important when I was with my uncle.

Now I am grown up and Uncle Carmine is an old, old man. I haven't seen him in years because I live far away from him now. But I always remember him walking up the hill from the train station carrying two large, round loaves of Italian bread wrapped in brown paper and tied together with a string.

ACTIVITIES

1. *Retelling*. Using your own words, tell your partner or group what you read about Uncle Carmine and about the storyteller.

2. Questions for comprehension:

   a. How old do you think the story teller was at the time he hunted with his Uncle Carmine?
   b. Why did the story teller look forward to his Uncle's visits?
   c. Why did the rabbit stew taste so good?
   d. What were some of the things that the story teller enjoyed about hunting with Uncle Carmine?
   e. Why didn't it matter to the story teller if they came back home empty-handed?
   f. Why was Uncle Carmine so important to the story teller?

3. Write about a relative or friend you were especially close to when you were younger (or are especially close to now). Describe in detail what you used to do together (or do now) with this person. Explain why this person was/is very important to you.

AIDA

Aida calls herself a "hair stylist." She cuts and styles men's hair in a "salon" on the second floor of a building on Broadway. She and her friend Caroline used to work together in another barber shop on Broadway, but they recently decided to open their own business.

Aida is about 50 years old and is an attractive woman. She came from Cuba fifteen years ago and speaks English with some difficulty and with a heavy accent. She prefers to speak Spanish. Caroline, who is young and who went to school in the United States, conducts most of the business with salesmen and the landlord.

Aida has two grown children, a son and a daughter. The son married when he was nineteen and now has a child of his own. He was in the army for three years, but now he is a civilian without a good profession or skill. Aida helps them as much as she can. She particularly likes her daughter-in-law, who was "just a baby" when she married. Aida's own daughter is twenty years old and is in her second year of college. Aida wants her to finish school before getting married. "Don't ruin your life like your brother did," she cautions.

Aida's family was well-off in Cuba. Her parents died when she was young and she was raised by her paternal grandparents. Her grandfather was a successful businessman who had been born in Cuba. But her grandmother came from Spain and thought she was "special." And she raised Aida to think that she was "special", too. Aida received a good education "for a girl" in those days (she finished high school), and she was raised to have absolute faith in God. She has a small sign on the wall near her barber's chair that reads, *Sin Dios, Nada; Con Dios, Todo.*

Aida's husband was a businessman like her grandfather, and when he came to the United States for better opportunities, she came with him, bringing her two small children. Her husband died and she had to support herself and her family, so she learned how to be a hair stylist.

Aida has a lot of customers, mostly businessmen, and you usually need an appointment to see her in the late afternoon or on Saturday. She is an excellent hair stylist.

ACTIVITIES

1. *Retelling.* Using your own words, tell your partner or group what you read about Aida.

2. Questions for comprehension:

   a. Why does Aida call herself a "hair stylist" instead of a "barber"?
   b. Why does Caroline conduct most of the business?
   c. Why does Aida want her daughter to finish school?
   d. Why did Aida's grandmother think it was "special" to have been born in Spain?
   e. Translate Aida's sign into English. Why do you think she keeps that sign on her wall?
   f. What do you like about Aida? What don't you like?
   g. Do you think Aida is a happy person? Explain why or why not.
   h. Why do you think Aida hasn't learned English very well?

3. Write about a person who came from another country to the United States as an adult. Use the following questions to help you and include any other information you would like to.

   a. Who is the person?

   b. When did he/she come to the United States?

   c. Why did he/she come to the United States?

   d. Did he/she have a family to take care of? A spouse? Children? Parents?

   e. Did he/she have to learn a new skill or profession? Describe it.

   f. How did the person learn English? In school? From reading? From television? From friends? on the job? Explain. Describe the person's ability to use English. Give examples.

   g. Is this person happy and leading a satisfying life? Would this person prefer to go back to his/her native country? Explain your answers and give specific examples of things that he/she says and does.

PAPA

Papa was coming. From the yard we could see him on his burro, slowly coming up the road. The girls ran to meet him, their mother and I following. When he saw us, he waved, stopped the burro, and waited. As we approached he lifted up his granddaughters one by one and hugged them warmly. Then it was his daughter Rosa's turn. The joy of seeing them again after so many months lit up his face. Finally a handshake for me as Rosa introduced me. Then, with one of the girls leading the burro, we walked back up the road to the house, Papa speaking quietly with Rosa all the while. As we went I couldn't help noticing his jet black hair, his deeply tanned skin, and his muscular build. But what attracted me most were his eyes, black but clear. It wasn't until later that I became aware of what I was seeing in those beautiful eyes.

Back home we sat down to dinner in the rapidly descending darkness. The meal—simple but delicious—reflected the simplicity and poverty of country people like Papa and his family. I spoke of my work as a teacher back in the United States. Papa, in a quiet, untroubled voice, spoke of his work in the fields as a sugar cane cutter. He worked seven days a week. From 7:00 in the morning 'til 7:00 at night he cut the cane with his machete under the tropical sun. He had to rise at 5:00 each morning to begin the long, slow journey to the fields on the hard back of his burro. His pay was very low. He didn't say so, but it was clear that he barely made enough to provide the necessities for his wife and younger children.

After supper Rosa, her younger sister, Papa and I played dominoes by lantern light and shared a bottle of good island rum that we had brought for Papa. His clear eyes laughed often in the lantern light. Our eyes often met and I unashamedly stared into his, fascinated.

The time to leave arrived too quickly. Papa and Mama both said that they were honored to have had me as their guest and they hoped that I had enjoyed their hospitality. I assured them that I had enjoyed myself very much and thanked them. As I shook Papa's hand good-bye, I looked one final time into his eyes. Then we left.

On the way back to Santiago I said very little to Rosa. I was thinking about Papa, trying to understand why he fascinated me. Finally it came to me. What I saw in Papa's eyes was peace. Papa was at peace with himself and his world. Even though he had to work incredibly hard and was incredibly poor, he had accepted all this as what was meant to be for him. He had found peace in the simplicity of his life and in his acceptance of it.

I began to think about my own life. I, a sophisticated, well-educated teacher from a big city with enough money to live well, had not found this inner peace. All my sophistication, all my education, and all my money could not bring it to me. I had been looking for it for many years but had not found it, had not even known how to find it. So Papa, who had nothing, was richer than I, who had a lot.

Then I began to see that things were backwards. Papa had said that he was honored to have me as his guest. But it should have been the other way around. I should have been the one honored to have met this simple man.

At the end of the summer I flew back to New York. Rosa stayed on her beautiful island with her children. I don't know if I will ever return. But whether or not I ever see Papa again, I know that I will never forget him.

ACTIVITIES

1. *Retelling*. Using your own words, tell your partner or group about Papa and why the storyteller was so impressed by him.

2. Questions for comprehension:

   a. Where does this story take place? How do you know?

   b. Describe Papa. What does he look like? What does he do? How does he feel about his life?

   c. What did the author see in Papa's eyes?

3. Write about someone (not related to you) whom you met and whom you admire very much. Explain what is special about this person. Is it attitude, personality, way of life? Tell what physical characteristics impressed you the most.

A FALLEN STAR REBOUNDS AT AGE 37

Gary Franks would dream of the game he loved and wake up with the knowledge that he had thrown it all away. "I would be back playing basketball," he said. "I could see the crowd. It would be real exciting."

For Franks, the memories carried added pain. He walked away from his chance at stardom at Auburn University in Alabama and gave up a possible professional career and a good education.

"I had been going to school for 12 years," Franks said. "I was tired of it. All I wanted was a car and some money." Franks settled for life in a small town and nearly 20 years of boring jobs.

But in 1986 Franks was back on the basketball court again. At age 37, he was playing for Albert Brewer Junior College. He was also on the dean's list.

Franks' body wouldn't do the things it used to, but he didn't care.

"For the first time in my life, I've set a goal for myself," he said. "I never did that before." His goal was to finally get that college degree and to be a college basketball coach.

The desire to change his life had been inside Franks for years, but it finally came out in 1985 when Franks and his wife Allison were driving back from an Auburn basketball game. As usual, Franks was complaining about the mistake he had made in his life.

Finally, his wife had enough. "I'm not going to waste my life watching you waste yours," said Mrs. Franks, an interior decorator. "I'll make the living if you go back to school."

He quit his job and enrolled at Brewer, a school of 600 students in Fayette, a small town about 100 miles northwest of Birmingham. He took 22 hours of classes a week.

Soon after enrollment, Franks found he was eligible to play on the basketball team and the coach was happy to give him a chance. Franks adopted a new diet, cutting down on the Pepsi that he drank all day long and eating more fruit. He began to work out. He read an instructional book on basketball. At night he went to the college gym and shot hundreds of free throws while his wife retrieved the balls. He got help from his nephew, a player on the high school team. He played in schoolyard games.

"It was a lot harder than I thought it would be," said Franks. "My legs would feel worn down like they were in mud." But when the 1985–86 season started, Franks was on the team.

Franks knew he couldn't go back in time, but once he was playing basketball again it became easier for him to think about the past. The year was 1967. Everybody was talking about Gary Franks, the greatest basketball player in Fayette history. He averaged 28 points and 14 rebounds a game. One night he scored 56 points, another night 54. "Gary had unlimited ability," said his high school coach. Except in the classroom.

Nothing changed when he arrived at Auburn. "Gary had a lot of ability, but just wouldn't go to school," said Bill Lynn, who was Auburn's head coach then. "He was immature. He didn't have any goals."

"When he dropped out of college," said his former high school coach, "a lot of people were disappointed in him. But now everybody is pulling for him again."

"I threw it all away," Franks said. "I made a mistake. But how many people get to correct their mistakes? How many people get a second chance?"

ACTIVITIES

1. *Retelling*. Using your own words, tell your partner or group Gary Franks' story.

2. Questions for comprehension:

a. The following words have a special meaning in the game of basketball. If you do not understand any of the words, try to find the appropriate meanings in a dictionary or ask someone in the class to explain them:

rebounds   free throws   passing   defensive

b. Write a sentence that illustrates the meaning of each of the following words or phrases as they are used in the story:

walked away from	cutting down
gave up	work out
settled for	dropped out
make the living	pulling for him

c. What two goals did Gary Franks set for himself at the age of 37?

d. What did he do to achieve these goals?

e. When Franks decided to try out for the basketball team, what did he do in preparation?

f. What risks did Gary Franks take?

3. Write about one of the following:

a. Describe a major risk that you have taken in your life. Tell what the risk was. Tell why it was a risk for you. Tell what happened. Tell how you feel about it now. Would you do it again if you had the chance?

b. Tell about something that happened in your life that you would like a "second chance" to do differently. Describe what happened. Tell what you would do differently. How would your life be different if you had that second chance? What would you have to do to get that second chance?

c. Tell about a difficult goal you set for yourself in the past. What was it? Tell specifically what you did to try to reach that goal. Did you reach it? Explain. If you did not, explain why. What would you do differently now?

PICTURE STORIES

PICTURE STORY NUMBER 1

Charles and Marsha have been friends for two years. They have just met on
the street. Something is wrong and they are talking about it.

ACTIVITIES

1. Discuss this picture with your partner or group. What do you think the problem is? What
   are they saying to each other?

2. Write about their conversation. Give the story a title.

PICTURE STORY NUMBER 2

José and Ramón are sitting at the table. Lisa is standing at the bar with her arms folded.

ACTIVITIES

1. Discuss this picture with your partner or group. Where is this bar located? Who are the people? Make up a story about them.

2. Write the story. Give it a title.

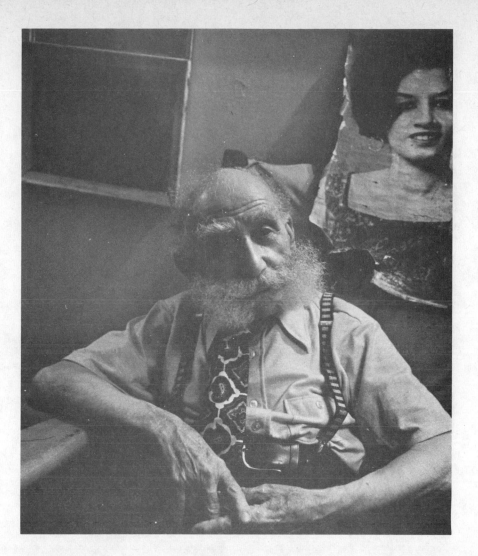

PICTURE STORY NUMBER 3

ACTIVITIES

1. Discuss this picture with your partner or group. Who is this man? Where is he? Who is the woman in the picture? What is he thinking about?

2. Write about this man. Give your story a title.

PICTURE STORY NUMBER 4

ACTIVITIES

1. Discuss this picture with your partner or group. Who is this girl? Where is she? What is she doing? What is she thinking about?

2. Write about this girl. Give your story a title.

MOVING ON

PET PEEVES

We all have our pet peeves, things that other people do that irritate or bother us. Some people don't like the physical habits of others, such as chewing gum, cracking knuckles, or biting nails. Others are bothered by signs of insincerity: people who don't pay attention to them when they are introduced; people who say, "We must get together sometime," but who don't mean it. Others are bothered by unintentional but serious matters of personality: someone who is always late or someone who doesn't keep promises or fulfill obligations.

And then there are those who have prejudices—unfair ways of thinking about and behaving toward certain groups of people, such as the attitudes some men have about women. This can be expressed in different ways; for example, treating a woman as though she were incompetent or a child. I was in a liquor store one day and witnessed the following: a young woman, obviously over 21, asked for a bottle of wine. "Are you sure you are old enough?" asked the man behind the counter teasingly. She replied angrily, "If I were a man, you wouldn't ask me that question." We all knew she was right.

ACTIVITIES

1. Questions for comprehension:
   a. Write a sentence that illustrates the meaning of each of the following words or phrases:

peeve	irritate	cracking knuckles
habit	prejudice	insincerity
tease	incompetent	unintentional

   b. List the four categories of peeves that the author describes. Under each category, write one example that the author gives and one example from your own experience.
   c. How did the woman know she was being teased? (Clue: If the store clerk really thought she was under 21, what question should he have asked?)

2. Describe a pet peeve of yours to your partner or group.

3. Write about your pet peeve. Describe it. Tell why it bothers you. Tell about a specific incident that illustrates it.

ALL IN THE FAMILY

Roger Lee, who came from Hong Kong when he was 7 years old, became the third member of his family to win a scholarship to Harvard University. His two older brothers had received the same honor before him. It is unusual for three brothers in the same family to achieve so highly, but it is not unusual to see so many Asian-Americans doing well academically.

Immigrants from all over the world tend to be highly motivated; they come to the United States to improve their lives and they work very hard at it. And because they have difficulties with English, many do well in science and math, which require less knowledge of English. And those who come from families in which the parents were well-educated in their native country have a background of respect for education.

But why is it that Asian-Americans in particular appear to be achieving so well academically? Social scientists, who study the behavior of large groups of people, say that Asian-Americans are no more intelligent than other groups. However, they possess a very strong sense of family, of achieving for the sake of the family and bringing it honor, pride, and a sense of accomplishment. Asians tend to work harder because the family expects it. According to one professor, most American mothers are happy if their children are a little above average, but Asian mothers expect their children to be the best.

Roger Lee's parents don't take much credit for their children's success. "We encouraged them to respect honesty and hard work, much the same as Western parents," says Roger's father.

"We just tried to give them the opportunity to learn," says his mother. Roger says his two older brothers gave him a great deal of help and encouragement.

Even if Roger's family won't take credit for his success, Roger gives them the credit and is working hard to make them proud of him.

ACTIVITIES

1. Questions for comprehension:

   a. Write a sentence to illustrate the meaning of each of the following words:

   | finalist | motivated | academically |
   | achieve | environment | encouragement |

   b. Where is Hong Kong?

   c. List three reasons given by the author for the success of many immigrants in the United States.

2. With your partner or group, tell about one person you know from another country who has been successful. What factors contributed to his or her success? Tell about your own family. How did your parents or other relatives influence you? If you have children or younger relatives, how are you trying to help them?

3. Write about one of the following:

   a. How can parents (and other relatives) help children be successful in school and in other aspects of their lives? What things should parents not do?

   b. American youngsters may behave differently from young people in your country. How would you help a young person in your family keep the values you think are important, yet become a part of American life? How have you done that for yourself?

GROWING UP AND PARENTING

ACTIVITIES

1. Discuss the questions below with your partner or group.

2. Write about growing up and parenting. Your composition will have three parts:

Part 1: **YOUR UPBRINGING**

Where were you raised? Who raised you? How were you raised? What were you allowed to do by yourself? What were you forbidden to do? What did you have to do? Were you given many things (toys, clothes, etc.)? Were you given love? How was this shown to you? Give other details and examples that show how you were raised.

Part 2: **YOUR FEELINGS ABOUT YOUR UPBRINGING**

What are your feelings about the way you were raised? What do you like and dislike about the way you were raised? Explain your feelings in detail.

How are your personality and behavior a result of the way you were raised?

Part 3: **PARENTING**

Answer one of the following sets of questions:

a. *If you have young children,* how are you raising them? Are you raising them in the same way you were raised? If yes, explain in detail. If no, explain how and why you are raising them differently.

b. *If you already have grown children,* how did you raise them? In the same way you were raised? Why or why not? What did you do that was right? What did you do that was wrong? Overall, are you satisfied with the way your children turned out? Be specific.

c. *If you don't have children yet,* how do you plan to raise your children in the future? In the same way you were raised? If yes, explain in detail. If no, explain how and why you would raise them differently.

d. *If you don't plan to have children,* what advice would you give to parents about raising children? Give examples from your own upbringing and your observation of others.

BRIEF ENCOUNTER

"Are you going to 181st Street?" asked an old woman.

The younger woman leaving the supermarket at 179th Street was in a hurry, but she stopped and turned to look. She saw an old lady leaning against the supermarket wall with a small bag of groceries at her feet. She was breathing hard.

"If you're going toward 181st Street, could you carry my bag for me?"

The woman hesitated for just a moment. "I don't have the time for this," she thought. She looked at the old woman, bent over and tired, and said, "Of course."

The old woman took hold of her companion's arm and they walked together slowly and talked. They were neighbors but they didn't know each other. The old woman lived alone and the younger woman lived with her family. They talked about the difficulty of living in a big city: the younger woman talked about the cost of food and the problems of raising children, the older about loneliness.

They finally reached the old woman's apartment house. She seemed reluctant to go in. She reached into her purse. "Let me give you a dollar for your trouble," she said.

"Oh, no. It was no trouble."

"Well, we're neighbors," the old woman said. "We'll see each other again."

"I hope so."

The old woman took her package and started to go in. Then she turned and said sadly, "But then, perhaps we'll never see each other again."

ACTIVITIES

1. With your partner or group, tell about a similar situation that you have been involved in or know about. How do you feel about helping an older/younger/handicapped person?

2. Write about a similar incident that you experienced with an older or younger or handicapped person.

3. Write about one of the following:

   a. How you would like to live when you are much older.

   b. How you would take care of your elderly parents or relatives in the future, or how you are taking care of them now.

   c. How people can overcome loneliness or handicaps.

   d. What should we (society) do to help old and handicapped people?

A TAILOR'S TALE

Angelo Litrico was born to a poor family in Sicily, but by the time he was 35 years old he had become the favorite menswear designer of many world leaders and show business personalities.

He learned to cut and sew clothes when he was a young boy, but as a teenager he knew he would not be satisfied to remain a tailor all his life in his small town of Catania.

At the age of 17 he traveled to Rome, arriving with less than $5 in his pocket. He went to work for a tailor and spent several years learning about and sewing fashionable clothing for the wealthy men of Rome. Eventually he decided to go into business for himself. For a while he had very few customers. Then one day, a friend gave him a ticket for the opera. To dress properly for the occasion, Angelo designed and sewed a new dinner jacket for himself. During intermission at the opera, Angelo started a conversation with the Italian actor, Rossano Brazzi, who admired his jacket and asked the name of his tailor. Angelo became Brazzi's tailor and soon he was designing clothes for other famous people.

In 1957, the first Italian fashion show traveled to the Soviet Union and Mr. Litrico went with it. He took along a camel's hair overcoat he had made as a present for Nikita Khrushchev, the Soviet leader. Khrushchev liked the coat and gave Litrico his measurements and his first order for two more overcoats, two suits, six ties, three hats, and two pairs of shoes. It was one of these shoes that Khrushchev banged on the table in a famous incident at the United Nations in 1960.

Khrushchev fell from power, but Litrico went on to greater success, designing clothes for other world leaders, including Presidents Eisenhower and Kennedy, British Prime Minister Harold Macmillan, Yugoslav President Tito, and Emperor Hirohito of Japan. Litrico accomplished a lifelong ambition first thought of when he was a young tailor's apprentice in a small town in Sicily.

ACTIVITIES

1. Discuss with your partner or group:

   a. What personality traits did Angelo Litrico possess that led to his success?

   b. What part did luck play in his success?

2. Write about one of the following:

   a. Tell about a successful person you know of who came from humble origins (a poor background). What contributed to his or her success?

   b. What are the three most important elements of personal success? Tell why you think each of these is important. Give examples.

WHY DID YOU BECOME AN ESL TEACHER?

Why did you become an ESL teacher? Students have asked me that from time to time. They think they are asking one question, but in fact they are asking two: Why did I become a teacher?, and why did I decide to teach ESL?

The first question is more difficult to answer. I did not start out to be a teacher. I was an editor and writer for a while and was not satisfied with the jobs I had. I had been an English major in college and wanted to work with the English language in some way. So I tried teaching and found that I liked it.

When I decided to study for a doctorate in order to teach in college, I needed a specialty, and teaching English to nonnative speakers seemed very appealing. First of all, I enjoy reading, listening to, and using the English language. Secondly, my father came to the United States from another country when he was 20 years old and often told me about his early experiences learning English and adjusting to life in a new country. So I always felt sympathetic toward people who had come from abroad. And I've always loved to travel and learn about other countries and other people's cultures.

So teaching English as a second language has given me the opportunity to meet interesting people and to help them lead better lives. I'm doing what I like, earning a good living, and helping people at the same time. Can you ask for a better job than that?

ACTIVITIES

1. Discuss with your partner or group:

   a. Would you like to be a teacher? Why or why not? If yes, what would you like to teach?

   b. Think of a job that you have had and tell what you liked and didn't like about it.

   c. What kind of job would you like to have in the future? Explain.

2. Write your opinion: What are the three most important things to look for in a job? Explain why each is important. Give examples from your own experience or the experience of others.

RESTORING HISPANIC THEATER IN THE BRONX

As a boy growing up in the late 1940's and early 50's, James Sanchez regularly attended shows at the Teatro Puerto Rico in the South Bronx, never dreaming that some day he would own it.

"My parents would take me here almost every Saturday," Mr. Sanchez recalled. "There would be a variety show and two movies, and sometimes my father would give somebody an extra dollar or two so we could sit down front."

In those days, the 2,700 seat theatre was a showcase for leading Spanish-speaking performers such as Mexico's Cantinflas, Cuba's Tres Patines, Puerto Rico's Iris Chacon, and many mariachi, rhumba and merengue bands.

The theater offered bargain entertainment for the city's Spanish-speaking population, but it was important for another reason. For young Hispanic New Yorkers growing up in the city's "Anglo" environment, the theater was a symbol of "hispanidad"—an affirmation of Hispanic culture and identity.

The theatre closed in the early 70's because of rising costs and because a lot of people were staying home and watching Spanish-language television.

Mr. Sanchez was born in Caguas, Puerto Rico, but came to New York at a young age and attended city public schools and New York University. Then he went into the real estate business and opened his own company in 1975.

He bought and renovated the building in 1984. It now has two movie theatres of 300 seats each, one occupying what was the balcony of the original theater.

"It's something the area needs," said Mr. Sanchez. "It will be one more step toward bringing the area back and stabilizing the neighborhood."

James Sanchez is glad he could give something back to the community that gave him so much.

ACTIVITIES

1. With your partner or group, tell George Lopez's story. What did he do for his community? Why?

2. Write a sentence using each of the following words to show that you understand its meaning:

variety show	showcase	affirmation
real estate	renovated	stabilizing

3. Write about one of the following:

   a. A public place (theater, museum, park, stadium) that you went to often when you were growing up. Describe the place and what you usually saw and did there. Tell why you enjoyed it and why it was important to you.

   b. George Lopez wanted to give something back to his community. What would you like to do for the community you grew up in? Tell in detail what you would do and how it would benefit the community.

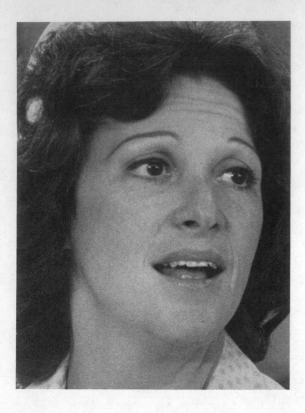

90

INTERACTING

Linda Lavin, the actress who appeared as the mother in Neil Simon's play "Broadway Bound," and as a waitress in the TV series "Alice," finds that her life and her art often interact. As a result of her TV role she joined the National Commission on Working Women, an organization that collects information and makes recommendations to the government regarding laws to help working women. The stepmother of two children, she made a TV movie about stepparenting and joined the Stepfamily Association of America. "Combining my life and my work helps me feel good," she says. "It also makes me a better person and a better actress."

On a flight from London to New York in 1953, Danny Kaye, the famous entertainer, met the Director of UNICEF, the United Nations Children's Fund. When he learned about UNICEF's work, Kaye felt that he had to help. For thirty-four years he worked for a cause that he believed in. He traveled thousands of miles around the world to bring laughter and joy to the young, and through his personal appeals persuaded millions of people to help UNICEF. Some people felt that the amount of time he spent on this effort took away from his career, and that he never reached his full potential as a performer. He said, "The greatest natural resource any country can have is its children, and UNICEF responds to the needs of children around the world. My long association with that agency has been the most rewarding and satisfying experience of my life."

ACTIVITIES

1. Discuss with your partner or group:

   a. Do you know about any other famous personalities (in show business, sports, art, business) who have used their talent and/or their fame to help needy people?

   b. Why did Lavin and Kaye give their time to help certain organizations?

2. Write: How can "ordinary" people use their talents to help others? Tell about yourself or other people you know about.

MELTING POT

Which works best for non-English-speaking students: continued instruction in their native language or immersion in English? Research results are inconclusive. Because no one is sure, the government has funded alternative programs, allowing local school boards and communities to decide what is best for their school children. However, this flexibility does not relieve school districts of their obligation to educate their students as effectively as possible. The Supreme Court has ruled that failure to provide such students some instruction in their native languages can deny them equal educational opportunity.

Whatever the approach, most people agree that a major goal should be to help children become proficient in English as quickly as possible. The Secretary of Education said recently that American citizens must share a "common language in which to discuss our common affairs." He and others suggest that the English language is the "melting pot" that brings people of many different backgrounds together as Americans. Failure to speak and understand English, they say, limits any citizen's ability to participate in American life.

ACTIVITIES

1. With a group, discuss one of the following topics. One student will write down the main points of agreement and disagreement in the group. When you have finished, share your ideas with the rest of the class.

   a. Do you agree with the ideas of the Secretary of Education? Is it possible to participate fully in American life without a good knowledge of English? Can someone be "successful" without knowing English very well? Give examples from your own experience and the experience of others you know or have heard about.

   b. What do you think is the best way for schoolchildren from other countries to learn English? Give examples from your own experience or the experience of others.

   c. Suggest the best methods you know of for adults to learn English. Give examples from your own experience or the experience of others.

   d. Should a school permit students to take courses such as history and art in their native language while they are learning English? Give reasons why or why not.

2. Choose one of the questions discussed above and write about it. Give your opinion, then give reasons to support that opinion.

TO SUFFER A LONG ILLNESS OR ELECT TO DIE

When Robert Bauer made his regular visit to his wife's hospital bedside one morning last year, he had no idea what was about to happen. For two years his wife, Emily, had suffered from amyotrophic lateral sclerosis, a gradual, incurable disease of the spinal cord that results in complete paralysis and eventual death. It is also called Lou Gehrig's disease, named after a famous New York Yankees baseball player who died of it.

She could not talk any more. She had a screen on her table and a switch by her pillow, which she could push with her head to print out a typed message.

Mrs. Bauer could not swallow, so tubes up her nose carried food to her stomach. She could not breathe by herself, so a respirator pumped air into her lungs through a hole in her throat. She could not control other body functions, either.

She had been determined to beat the disease, but that morning she began to tap out a message to her husband. "I want to die."

Mrs. Bauer had first developed the disease three years earlier. It started as a small paralysis in her right foot and gradually spread up her leg. She was a counselor and a teacher, and she continued her work during the first year of her illness. Even though she went from cane to crutches, then to a walker, a wheelchair and then a motorized wheelchair, Mrs. Bauer talked of recovery someday. The Bauers followed her doctor's advice. They also visited faith healers. She took huge doses of vitamins. They prayed. Nothing helped.

To pay for treatments they sold their country house and moved into an apartment close to a hospital. Robert began spending less time at work and more at home, caring for two demanding children in one room and a demanding sick person in the other. He felt occasional anger at his situation, but said nothing. Then one day, Emily began gasping for breath.

"This could be it," he told her. "What do you want to do?"

"I'll make every effort to live," she whispered.

He rushed her to the hospital and she was put on a respirator, a machine that would breathe for her for the rest of her life. From then on he would visit her every day. Every week he took the children there. They would sit in their mother's lap and hug her, although she could show no response except some tears.

During the hours she was alone in the hospital, Emily used the switch by her pillow to tap out, letter by letter, fanciful stories for her daughters about two butterflies named Jill and Lisa who travelled in the sky on rainbows and moonbeams. And each night, Robert would sit by his children's beds and read them the latest happy adventure. The next day in the hospital, he would tell his wife about the children's reactions to her stories. Her eyes would grow wide and bright when she heard how much her daughters enjoyed them.

Emily tapped out other stories for the hospital psychologist, details of her thoughts, feelings and dreams. After five months in the hospital, those feelings and dreams started becoming angry and afraid. She was terrified of falling into a coma and staying that way for years. She knew she was getting worse and had given up hope of beating the disease.

Then one day she tapped out the message for her husband, telling him that she wanted to die. Mr. Bauer told her: "I don't know what to do. I love you. I can't kill you." But she insisted that she wanted to die.

Robert hired a lawyer and they discussed the matter with Emily's doctor and psychologist. Emily tapped out a message in front of them saying she wanted to die. Finally, after months of discussion with Emily's doctors, nurses, psychologist, and a law-enforcement officer, the hospital sent her home for a day with only a portable respirator. The children, who had seen their mother a few days before, were visiting relatives. A few close friends came over for lunch and then left. Robert talked to Emily about the future, what kind of people they wanted their children to be. They agreed it was the end of the path they had started together. She just wouldn't be there for the rest of the journey. The doctor came in and gave her an injection to make her sleep. Robert disconnected the air tubes, as he had been instructed. "And then an incredible thing happened," said Robert. "She opened her eyes and moved her lips to say 'Thank you.'"

ACTIVITY

Discuss with a group: Did Robert Bauer do the right thing in helping his wife to die? Give your reasons.

The story about Robert and Emily Bauer is true, although the names are different. As a result of Emily's illness, the Bauers spent all their money on medical expenses and Robert was left with a debt of $35,000.

It is estimated that every year thousands of sick people in the United States arrange for their own deaths or have them arranged by relatives. This is a situation that has developed in recent years as a result of advanced medical technology, which is prolonging the lives of people who previously would have died as the result of certain diseases and injuries. This practice often results in physical suffering for the patient, emotional suffering for the relatives, and great financial cost to individuals and to society.

Many doctors and hospital administrators say that it is their responsibility to keep people alive as long as possible. It is against the religious beliefs of many people to take a human life, even to end a person's suffering. And it is against the law. Some doctors, nurses, and others have been punished for helping to end a sick person's life.

However, in a famous case in New Jersey, a judge permitted the parents of a young woman, who had been in a coma for ten years, to take her out of the hospital and to let her die at home. The family priest urged the judge to allow it. Two district attorneys in the New York area said they would not prosecute anyone involved in a "negotiated death" unless they received a complaint.

A young woman whose elderly mother and father died within two years of each other told this story:

When my mother got sick she went to the hospital. The doctors knew they couldn't cure her, but they kept her alive for three months with machines. She lay in bed for three months with tubes in her nose and mouth and arms. She suffered. My father and I suffered. A year later, when my father got sick I kept him home. He had his own bright, sunny room and his own bed, and I took care of him. He died, but he died with dignity. That's the way I want to die, at home, with dignity.

Committees of doctors and lawyers are developing guidelines on when it is appropriate to end medical care. Individuals are writing "living wills" telling what they would want done if they were ever to suffer from an incurable disease.

ACTIVITIES

1. Discuss the following questions with other members of your class:

   a. Should people with incurable illnesses be allowed to die if they want to?

   b. Should people in comas who have suffered irreversible brain damage be permitted to die if their closest relatives request it? Give reasons and examples from situations you know about personally or have read about.

2. Write a "living will." In the will, tell how you would want to be treated if you had an incurable illness or if you were in a coma.

3. Write your opinion: Should laws be changed to allow people to negotiate their own deaths? Why or why not? Give reasons. If you think negotiated death should be allowed, be specific about the conditions.

FROM TEACHER TO TEACHER

We have been around long enough to remember when the word "traditional," applied to English language teaching, meant the teacher standing at the blackboard in front of rows of obedient (that is, quiet) students teaching grammar. "Teaching grammar" usually meant writing "rules" on the board, giving examples, and then letting students practice at their seats with handout exercises or textbooks. In those days, a really sophisticated approach was the use of "sentence diagrams," in which subject and verb phrases were neatly dissected and underlined and modifiers were written tangentially beneath the main sentence parts. The assumption was that mastery of this kind of grammatical knowledge would automatically lead to better speaking and writing, and, besides, it was fun (for the teacher), an easy lesson to prepare and deliver, and student mastery was readily testable.

However, experience, supported by considerable research, taught us that students who learned grammar in this way did not necessarily write better. Even those who got consistently high grades on grammar tests would repeat the same mistakes over and over in their writing.

What to do? We sought new ideas, new methods, read the journals, attended conferences and workshops, and sat at the feet of gurus who promised salvation. As blackboards became green and were renamed "chalkboards" we also changed and slowly developed some basic principles for the teaching of language and, in particular, the teaching of writing to mature students. This is not to suggest that as we write these words in the fall of 1987 we possess the final truth. We learn more each day from our students and colleagues. But at this moment, *Put It in Writing* is our way of sharing our current thinking with our colleagues in the field.

Let's start with a few basic principles derived from experience and with considerable debt to Father Charles Curran's work as embodied in Counseling–Learning/Community Language Learning.

1. With appropriate guidance, security, and motivation, students at any level of proficiency can write meaningfully and well.

2. In most instances, students should have the opportunity to express their ideas orally before writing them.

3. Students learn and derive support from fellow students at least as much as from their instructor.

4. Students are more willing to express themselves through speaking and writing (that is, to take the risks involved) if they really want to communicate.

5. Students, at least initially, are most willing to talk and write about themselves and about people, experiences, and places that have personal meaning.

6. Once they have invested themselves in communicating through writing, students are ready and motivated to learn the technicalities of the language, that is, grammar, spelling, and so on.

In this book, we have put these principles into practice by providing activities that:

1. immediately engage students in speaking and writing;

2. are controlled enough to provide security and interesting enough to engage mature students;

3. require student interaction;

4. begin with personal writing, primarily narrative and descriptive, before moving on to the realm of ideas as expressed by expository writing; and

5. do not require previous grammatical instruction.

In the classroom, we have put our principles into practice by, among other things, eliminating the "front of the room." The focus is not on the location of the chalkboard or the position of the teacher. Typically, students in our classes sit in a circle, in pairs, or in clusters, and the teacher acts primarily as a facilitator. This requires a room with movable desks and a teacher with considerable patience and self-control. Also required is a knowledge of students' abilities, and the time and energy to individualize, providing particular students, or groups of students, with appropriate activities.

As teachers, we have found it better to subordinate teaching to learning, and formal grammar to communication; to constantly reassess our students' abilities; to avoid preconceptions, allowing students to begin at their own beginning rather than ours; and to be accepting, creating an atmosphere in which students are willing to take risks. Now let us be specific about *Put It in Writing*.

HOW TO USE THIS BOOK

Start at the beginning with "Profile." It's visual; it's entertaining; it allows students to introduce themselves to each other and to the instructor; it can be serious or humorous; it asks initially for a written outline; and it will provide you with a written paragraph for evaluation at the end of the first class session. Our suggestion for this and the first few compositions submitted to you is not to give a letter grade or mark the paper extensively with corrections. An eminent teacher of teachers once remarked that the traditional red marking pencil liberally applied to a student's paper suggested a bloody dissection and was bound to be debilitating, if not fatal. A green pen or ordinary pencil used sparingly, and initially only for a positive comment, would probably be less painful and more helpful to students at this point.

At the next session, you might be in a position to pair students in a meaningful way, for example, two students with different strengths. One might have a reasonable command of structure and the other good idiomatic usage. (More later about evaluating student writing.) Ask them to help each other make corrections while you circulate to give assistance as needed. Another effective although more time-consuming method is to have groups of four to six students correcting portions of each other's papers either written on the board or with marking pens on large sheets of newsprint taped to the classroom walls. As a follow-up writing exercise, students can move on to items 3 and 4 of "Profile," the results of which will provide you not only with more information about your students' writing skills but also tell you something about their goals in life. Both will be valuable in helping you plan succeeding activities.

SEQUENCING

This book contains six types of activities, grouped as follows:

1. Semi-controlled Writing

2. Story completion

3. Model compositions

4. Dialogue writing

5. Writing in response to a story

6. Writing in response to a picture

7. "Moving On," a final section that incorporates most of these types but demands a more sophisticated response, usually in expository writing.

The selections have been sequenced more or less according to the amount of reading involved, the length of the writing required by the activity, and the amount of control built in. For example, the semi-controlled writing selections come before the less controlled dialogues; within the semi-controlled selections, "A Difficult Decision" comes before "The Fire" because it requires only three paragraphs and is more tightly controlled. However, the selections do not have to be used in order either according to categories or within categories. Generally speaking, the less proficient students will begin with the shorter, easier, more controlled activities, but sometimes even relatively advanced writers can benefit from some of the more controlled work. While the sequencing reflects the difficulty of each category as a whole, individual activities within any of the first three sections may be easy enough for lower-level students to attempt at or near the beginning of a course. Selections from sections 4 through 7 and some from 1 through 3 become appropriate at that point in the course when students have demonstrated that they are ready for the longer, more difficult activities. Students in the high-intermediate to low-advanced range could conceivably function almost anywhere in the book. If your classes are anything like ours, you will find a wide range of abilities among your students. To the extent that your time and energy allow, try to tailor the activity to the individual student, or groups of students, rather than having the entire class march together from cover to cover.

There is another aspect to sequencing. We believe that speaking should precede writing in order to give students the opportunity to develop their ideas and verbalize certain structures and vocabulary that they will want to use in their writing. Once again, this is not to be seen as an opportunity for the instructor to push a particular grammatical point but rather to respond when appropriate to the students' desire to communicate effectively.

We also begin with personal writing, primarily narrative and descriptive, to give students the opportunity to write about what they know and care most about. When they achieve a degree of confidence and proficiency, they will then be more willing to "move on" to the greater demands of expository writing required in the last section.

In the following section we briefly state the purpose of each section of the book and give step-by-step suggestions for using representative exercises in the earlier sections.

ACTIVITIES STEP BY STEP

Section/Selection	Procedure	Grouping
SEMI-CONTROLLED WRITING	As we have stated, this book seeks to offer activities that students can invest in, while providing security through varying degrees of control. It is in this section that we provide the most control. It is a good starting point because it will enable most students at the advanced beginning level and beyond to function comfortably and well while allowing the instructor time to evaluate an individual student's abilities. It is the instructor's responsibility to determine how long to keep particular students working in this section before moving them on to less controlled activities.	
Profile	1. Have students read advertisement aloud and help each other with comprehension. Ask questions to determine purpose of the piece and to find if students feel they know this person. What kind of person is he? What else would they like to know about him?	Whole Class
	2. Tell the students about yourself, using the categories listed in the activity. Write answers in short form on board.	Whole Class
	3. Ask students to tell each other about themselves and then write their own profiles in the form you have illustrated (Activity 1).	Pairs
	4. Ask students to exchange papers to check for any errors (such as spelling, verb forms). Be available to answer questions.	Pairs
	5. Ask students to write a paragraph about themselves using the profile information (Activity 2).	Individual
	6. Return papers. Ask students to rewrite their own papers or make corrections.	Individual
	7. Move on to Activities 3 and 4 as in steps 3–5 above.	Pairs and Individual
	8. Return papers as in 6 above.	Individual

Section/Selection	Procedure	Grouping
The Person Who Takes Care of Your Building	1. Introduce this by eliciting choices from students and writing the first few sentences on the board.	Whole Class
	2. Ask students to read the questions together and agree on answers. Then they write the composition together, each one writing the same thing on his or her paper.	Pairs
	3. Have students exchange papers to be sure their wording is identical and there are no errors.	Pairs
	4. Circulate and suggest changes as necessary.	Pairs
The Fortune Teller	1. Ask two students to join you in acting out this situation for the class. You play the fortune teller and predict what will happen to the second student. The third student writes your remarks on the board. With the class, correct what has been written on the board. Or have two students join you as above. One student asks you questions about him/herself from text. You respond as the fortune teller. The second student writes your responses on board. Class corrects together.	Whole Class
	2. Ask all students to act out the situation. Circulate and provide help as necessary (Activity 1).	Pairs
	3. Ask students to write what the fortune teller said about them. They may write what the partner said or, if they prefer, they may decide the information for themselves (Activity 2).	Individual
	4. Have students exchange papers for correction.	Pairs
	5. Have the more advanced students write this story in reported speech (Activity 3). Other students may return to this activity later in the semester.	Individual
	6. During the self-correction process you may refer them to the examples at the end of the selection.	Pairs or Individual
A Letter Home	A suitable homework or individual classroom assignment.	
The Fire	1. Ask students to describe to each other a fire that they saw.	Pairs or Group (4–6 students)
	2. Those students who have a vivid memory of a fire may be asked to write about it immediately.	Individual
	3. Those students who have not seen a fire recently or who, in your opinion, need more structure for this exercise should be paired and instructed to write together by answering the questions.	Pairs
	4. All students should exchange papers for help with correction before checking by the instructor.	Pairs

Section/Selection	Procedure	Grouping
A Lecture	1. Ask students to exchange opinions on questions in parts a and b.	Whole Class
	2. Break into appropriate groupings and have students discuss remaining questions (Activity 1). Circulate to assist as needed.	Pairs or Group
	3. Have students write the lecture, responding to as many of the questions as they can work with comfortably (Activity 2). (For example, encourage those whom you think are underproducing to write more.)	Individual
	4. After self-correction, elicit possible ways to begin a lecture. Then ask students to write an introduction to their lectures.	Whole Class
	5. After suitable revisions, volunteers can read their lectures to the class and then respond to questions.	Whole Class
	6. Have more advanced students respond to Activity 3. You may add other topics suggested by the questions.	Individual
STORY COMPLETION	This section typifies our effort to provide material that students can become involved with. In some cases, such as "The Lottery," students have found the story so compelling that they are eager to finish it immediately. We encourage them to do so without preliminary discussion. In other selections, such as "Grace's Dilemma," we feel that some whole class or group discussion is desirable because we are not dealing primarily with a story line but with values that we think can best be explored through an interaction in which students share opinions and personal experiences before writing.	
The Lottery	1. Read the story aloud. Ask students to reread the story and then to write the conclusion immediately.	Individual
	2. After the writing and correction activities, have students work on Activities 2 and 3.	Pairs or Group
	3. Follow up with Activity 4.	Individual
Out of Gas	Ask students to write this story individually or in pairs, depending on their level of independence at this point.	Individual or Pairs
An Unforgettable Night	1. Ask students to read the story by themselves and then break into groups to respond to Activity 1.	Pairs or Group
	2. Students write the conclusion. Male students may choose to write from Bill's point of view.	Individual
	3. Refer students to examples of direct and indirect speech as necessary during the correction process.	Individual
	4. Assign Activity 3 to those students whom you judge capable of handling the conditional. You may assign this activity later in the semester to other students as they become more proficient.	Individual

Section/Selection	Procedure	Grouping
MODEL COMPOSITIONS	Models can be used in two ways: as specific, controlled guides for students to follow closely, as they may do with "Interview with Kenneth" and "A Letter of Complaint," or as springboards to original writing, perhaps encouraged most by "Anecdote" and "The Barber Shop." At this point, the instructor should have a sense of student potential and encourage students to "stretch" themselves, that is, write with as much originality as you think they can manage rather than taking the easiest route of rewriting a selection. ("Interview with Kenneth" may be suitable as a follow-up to "Profile" early in the semester, with the sample questions and answers used, if necessary.)	
DIALOGUES	The dialogues may be difficult to intiate, but once understood by the students they are among the most popular and rewarding activities in the book. Initially, active participation by the instructor is desirable.

Please note: The value of the dialogues lies in their not being problem-solving activities. The people in the dialogue situations are not problems, nor do they have problems for which the students are to supply the answers. They are real people in conflicts for which there may or may not be solutions. For example, in "Anna and Martin," the final statement in students' role playing or dialogue writing may be something like this: "I'm not satisfied. We'll have to talk about this again." Or in "Luisa Rodriguez," an ending may be: "Okay, I'll obey you because you're my mother, but I'm not happy." On the other hand, partial solutions are sometimes found, such as Mrs. Rodriguez's suggesting that Luisa invite her boyfriend home to dinner, or Martin's decision to give up gambling. Sometimes the conflict is resolved completely. Rather than "problem solving," what engages the students in the dialogue writing are the values involved in the situation: love and respect for one's parent or spouse versus the desire for freedom and independence; the desire to live one's own life; to feel worthwhile, etc. | |
Luisa Rodriguez and her Mother	1. Read the story aloud, with the instructor and students taking turns.	Whole Class
	2. Ask volunteers to retell the story to the class. Give students the opportunity to add information or to ask questions (Activity 1).	Whole Class
	3. Demonstrate the procedure with a student. You take the role of mother or older brother and ask a female student to take the role of Luisa. Ask "Luisa" to begin the conversation as written and continue, keeping in character.	Whole Class

Section/Selection	Procedure	Grouping

4. Pair students (Activity 2). Partner selection is perhaps more important here than in most activities. Do not pair two males for this one. Where you have a male and female paired, substitute "Luisa's older brother" for her "mother" (Activity 4.)   **Pairs**

5. Supervise closely as students write Activity 3, helping them to follow the direct speech format illustrated in the book.   **Pairs**

READ AND WRITE

The primary purpose of the selections in this section is to elicit the reader's identification with the story teller or situation and thereby to stimulate thinking and writing on similar themes. Therefore, in supervising the retelling and question activities, look for recognition of feelings, as well as seeing that students understand the stories and recognize the importance of details in telling a comprehensible story. We have been surprised, sometimes overwhelmed, by the quality and emotional content of the writing inspired by the selections in this section. Many students find themselves deeply engaged in these activities and seem to take extra care with their work. In sum, this section has provided us with more productive discussion and quality writing than we might have anticipated.

PICTURE STORIES

While some structure has been provided for each of the pictures, students should be given wide latitude in interpreting them. The pictures are of most value when they evoke personal recognition.

MOVING ON

In this section we offer several readings and exercises designed to stimulate thinking and written exposition on important themes. We begin with "Pet Peeves," which can be used as a springboard for consideration of such issues as treatment of women and minorities; and continue with child-rearing and the establishment of values in children in "All in the Family" and "Parenting"; caring for the elderly in "Brief Encounter"; careers and the meaning of success in "A Tailor's Tale" and "Why Did You Become an ESL Teacher?"; community responsibility in "Restoring Hispanic Theater in the Bronx" and "Interacting"; and two current issues of controversy—bilingual education in "Melting Pot" and treatment of the incurably ill in "To Suffer a Prolonged Illness or Elect to Die."

The selections will give those students who are ready for expository writing an entry into the realm of ideas and controversy, beginning with some familiar and personal situations. It is here that the instructor is most encouraged to go beyond the book: to ask students to look for additional, relevant articles in newspapers and magazines, to help students distinguish between fact and opinion, and to introduce them, or reintroduce them, to the resources of the school library.

EVALUATING STUDENT WRITING

More and more educators involved in the evaluation of student writing are looking at "fluency"—the ability of the writer to produce a sustained composition that communicates adequately: that is, present a story or a point of view in a logical and understandable way. This suggests some sense of organization, sufficient information and detail, a reasonable vocabulary, and enough technical skill so as not to seriously distract the reader. Such a definition emphasizes communication and clarity, with accuracy a secondary, but not unimportant, issue. This view of writing is incorporated into "holistic" rating systems used by many educational institutions to evaluate writing. It is a method that asks the reader to read rather quickly for overall effect and to rate the composition on that basis rather than on number or type of errors.

We would like to suggest that this holistic approach is applicable and constructive in helping students to improve their writing ability. As we have mentioned, we tend to avoid the heavy marking of papers early in the semester. If the student has made an honest effort to communicate, we try to find something positive to say and perhaps make a suggestion or two for change. We look to see that students have understood the assignment, followed instructions, and communicated to the best of their ability at this point. When students have gained confidence in themselves and in us, we can begin to point out those matters of form that help or hinder the writer in communicating. But not all at once. We suggest establishing a hierarchy of concerns, beginning with one or two from a list that might include verb tense, paragraph form, end punctuation, plurals, and idiomatic usage, which limits understanding. Spelling, use of prepositions, word forms, dependent clause construction, dialogue form and indirect speech might be included in a second level of concern. One way to determine what is important in terms of accuracy is to read holistically, make an overall judgment, and then reread more carefully to see which types of errors contributed most to the judgment. This determination will vary from teacher to teacher, depending on individual sensibilities; but by comparing notes (that is, student compositions and your reactions to them) with colleagues, you can develop a consensus. Our extensive involvement in holistic readings over the years at the City University of New York has suggested the hierarchy indicated above.

Specific notations on student papers will depend on your knowledge of the individual's ability. Some students will need a word circled or underlined with a marginal abbreviation indicating type of error. Some will merely need the word underlined, or perhaps just a check in the margin next to the sentence containing an error. For some, you might only have to write a note at the top suggesting one type of error to be corrected (such as "All verbs should be in past.") For the best, you might only have to indicate number of errors at the top. But for all, it is not unreasonable to expect some degree of self-correction. Certain types of errors, particularly idiomatic and structural, may require a conference to help the individual with corrections. Periodic conferences with all students is of course desirable.

A word on grading: We prefer to postpone giving grades until the students have demonstrated their willingness to take risks, the result of an atmosphere of mutual trust. Grades should be seen not only as an institutional requirement but also as a way of evaluating individual progress. We do not grade students by some ideal standard but rather by degree of progress from beginning to now; from last assignment to this; by ability to correct previous errors; and by willingness to do more than the minimum—to take the risks necessary for language development. In short, we use grades to reward progress and risk-taking. And we also acknowledge that in grading compositions we rely to some extent on subjective judgment. The message is that we want to be fair and to be encouraging.

Which seems to us a good note on which to end this lengthy, but we hope useful, sharing of ideas. We are attaching a short list of readings that we have found helpful. We encourage you to take a look at our companion volume for beginning level ESL students, *Write from the Start,* and to share with us your ideas and your reactions to ours.

D.M.D.
D.B.

SUGGESTED READINGS

Curran, Charles A. *Counseling–Learning in Second Languages*. Apple River, Illinois: Apple River Press, 1976.
Mayher, John S. *et al. Learning to Write/Writing to Learn*. Upper Montclair, NJ: Boynton/Cook, 1983.
Stevick, Earl W. *Memory, Meaning and Method*. New York: Newbury House, 1976.
Stevick, Earl W. *A Way and Ways*. New York: Newbury House, 1980.